# ACCORDING
## to
# LUKE

Clare Richards

BLACKIE

Blackie & Son Ltd
Bishopbriggs, Glasgow G64 2NZ
7 Leicester Place, London WC2H 7BP

Richards, Clare
    According to Luke.
    1.  Bible. N.T. Luke—Commentaries
    I.  Title
    226'.406          BS2595.3

    ISBN 0-216-91990-8 Pbk
    ISBN 0-216-91989-4 E.Pbk

Printed in Great Britain by Bell & Bain (Glasgow) Ltd

# PREFACE

I have written this book on Luke's Gospel with examinations at 16+ in mind, but students of biblical studies at many levels and people in study groups will I hope find it interesting and helpful. Although it is primarily written for those studying Luke, since it frequently compares Luke with Matthew and Mark, it should also prove useful for those studying the Synoptic Gospels. My aim has been to bring to the students not only the traditional interpretation of the Gospel but also the results of recent New Testament scholarship.

I firmly believe that it is *not* the role of the Religious Studies teacher to present the Gospel in a confessional way for exam purposes. The GCSE examination is intended to be 'open to candidates of any religious persuasion or none'. I have, therefore, tried to write in as neutral and objective way as I can. Denominational schools may obviously wish to supplement what I have written but that is another matter.

The book is in three parts.

**PART A   Background** is a simplified background to New Testament times and to the Gospels in general. Teachers may wish to use it for reference.

**PART B   Luke's Story** is the core. It is a study of Luke's Gospel using the thematic approach, rather than a verse-by-verse, commentary. Each chapter is divided into four sections. The *first* 'The way in' introduces the theme. The *second* 'Main issues' contains the basic facts that all candidates will need. I introduce more complicated ideas in the *third* section, called 'Further issues'. Some of this material is difficult. I make no apology for this. In New Testament studies we are dealing with a theology that has exercised some of the best intellects over the centuries. To simplify overmuch can easily distort. Teachers will know how much of this material to use. The 'Questions and Things to Do' in the *fourth* section are designed to help students to know the text, as well as to understand the real meaning of what they are studying.

It is essential that students become familiar with the Gospel text itself. One way of ensuring this is to encourage them to re-read before questions are attempted. I have always found it helpful when students have their *own* copies of the Gospel. Then they can make margin notes as they wish. For example, it is a useful exercise to skim the Gospel and mark all the parables in one colour and all the miracles in another colour. I strongly recommend using the *Good News Bible* and all biblical quotations are from it.

**PART C** is called **Luke for Today**. Students need to see that Christians find the Gospel has something to say to today's world. This section ties in with the paper on Christianity and Life which is usually offered as an option in the syllabus. It is no way comprehensive but is intended as material for discussion and students may find it gives useful ideas for further projects.

# Acknowledgments

The author and publishers are grateful to the following
for permission to use copyright material:

**Text**

All the quotations from the Old and New Testa-
ments are from the *Good News Bible*, © American Bible
Society 1966, 1971, 1976 published by the Bible
Societies and Collins.

Oxford University Press for *The Pilgrim Song* by Percy
Dearmer page 45

Christian Aid for the Question and Answer extracts
pages 99, 103

TRO Essex Music Ltd for extracts from *Standing in
The Rain* by Sydney Carter pages 101, 103

Westminster Music Ltd for extract from *Streets of
London* by Ralph McTell page 101

SOS Kinderdorf International for extract on Hermann Gmeiner page 109

Peter De Rosa for the prayer page 115

Stainer & Bell Ltd for *Friday Morning* from 'Songs of
Sydney Carter in the Present Tense Book 2' page 120

**Photographs**

George Milward cover—top left, top right

Alfred Saffa cover—middle right

John Fanshawe cover—bottom left

Robert J Drake cover—bottom right, pages 2, 22,
100 middle and bottom left, 115

Musée des Beaux-Arts de Dijon page 3

Barbara Norris pages 7c, 20, 51 bottom, 55, 64
bottom

Ronald Sheridan's Photo Library pages 7e, 9, 10
bottom right, 13, 26, 43, 50, 51 top, 52, 53, 56, 58
top, 62, 76

BIPAC pages 10 bottom left, 98 bottom

Adam Green/BIPAC page 10 top

Genut Audio Visual Productions pages 11 bottom
left and bottom right, 110

The Weiner Library pages 12 top, 102 middle, 103
bottom

UNRWA pages 12 bottom, 16, 33, 34, 57, 82, 90,
95, 99 bottom, 112 top

Eastern Daily Press pages 14, 25, 116, 117 bottom

USPG page 28

Smith and Nephew Consumer Products Ltd page 31

University of East Anglia, Photographer Alan
Howard page 35

Scottish Television and Church of Scotland Lodg-
ing House Mission Committee page 37

Kairos page 45

Bantam Press page 47

World Council of Churches pages 49 left, 69, 104,
114

Pamela Carter pages 49 right, 67 top

The British Museum pages 58 bottom, 59f

Victoria and Albert Museum page 59a

The Mansell Collection Ltd pages 59b, 65, 80
bottom

Markt- Drogerie Foto-Haus page 59c

Commissioners of Public Works, Ireland page 59d

The Art Institute of Chicago page 59e

Bill Sinclair page 60

John Fisher pages 67 bottom, 83, 100 bottom right

Mary Anne Felton pages 72, 98 top, 107 bottom
right, 119 top

Esther Fitzmaurice cover—top middle, page 80 top

The Fotomas Index Library page 85

Fitzwilliam Museum page 87

Glen Edwards page 88

Syndication International pages 99 top, 103 middle, 105 bottom, 106, 107 top, 111 top, 117 top

ROSPA page 100 top

Topham Picture Library page 101 top

NSPCC page 101 bottom

Jon Wyand page 102 top

Link page 102 bottom

Amnesty International page 103 (postcard), 105
top

Monsignor Bruce Kent page 107 left

The Leonard Cheshire Foundation page 107 middle
right

SOS Kinderdorf International page 109 top

BJ Rampley page 109 middle

David Richardson page 109 bottom

Popperfoto page 111 bottom

Glasgow Herald page 112 bottom

Patrick Brady page 113 left

Our Lady of the Wayside, Solihull page 113 right

Brian Avis, Duncan Paul Associates page 119
bottom

Quaker Peace and Service page 119 (co-operation
illustration)

Any photograph not acknowledged above was
supplied by the author.

Drawings and maps by the author, except page 27
which was drawn by the author's daughter, Blanca.

# Contents

Part A

# Background

# A1 What this book is about

There is probably no one in the whole history of mankind who has had so much written about him as Jesus of Nazareth. He has not only been written about; throughout the ages artists have painted him and musicians have been inspired to compose great works in his honour. In our own times films and musicals are produced about him. Why should this be? Who was he?

Jesus was a first century Jew whose life was not very remarkable. He was born to a peasant woman in Palestine, in a village in the back of beyond. For most of his life he worked as a carpenter. For three years he was a wandering preacher with a message that made him increasingly unpopular. In the end even his friends left him. His short life was very ordinary but his death was dramatic. After an absurd trial he was given the death sentence and hanged on a cross between two criminals.

Every day hundreds of ordinary people meet tragic deaths. Why is Jesus of Nazareth remembered when they are forgotten? And why would Jesus be described by a writer in these words:

> All the armies that ever marched, and all the parliaments that ever sat, and all the kings that ever reigned, put together, have not affected the life of man upon the earth as has this one solitary life.
>
> *Bishop Phillips Brooks of Massachusetts 1835–93*

An ordinary man with an extraordinary influence upon the world—that is exactly how *Luke* saw Jesus. He was one of the earliest writers to offer an explanation.

Luke was an educated Greek doctor, interested in very ordinary people. He was a down-to-earth man himself.

In this book we are going to look at Jesus through his eyes.

An early icon of Luke

# A2 The Gospels

## Jesus the preacher

Jesus was a Jew of the first century (in fact we date our years from his birth). The Jews believed they were chosen by God to play a special role in the history of the world. At the time of Jesus it was not clear what this role ought to be. For the previous 90 years his country had been occupied by a foreign power—Rome. What did it mean to be 'God's people' in these circumstances?

Jesus had his own clear answer, and preached it fearlessly. He had a vision of God and his relationship to mankind that was to change the course of history.

## The followers of Jesus

Those who accepted this new vision of God could not help seeing the ordinary man who preached it as extraordinary. They called him *The Christ* (God's Chosen One), and were soon nicknamed 'Christians'. It was for these followers of Jesus that Luke wrote his book—to share with them what Jesus had come to mean for him.

## The early writings about Jesus

Christ preaching to the apostles, a 5th Century Byzantine ivory plaque (Musée des Beaux-Arts de Dijon)

Not much was written down about Jesus at first. Most people couldn't read. The best way to let people know about him was to *tell* them. After some years, sayings of Jesus and stories about him were written down in collections, especially for the instruction of new followers. These collections formed the basis of four books called the *Gospels*. They were written by Matthew, Mark, Luke and John. We call them *Evangelists*, meaning people who spread good news.

## What sort of writing is a Gospel?

The word 'gospel' (Anglo-Saxon 'god-spell') means 'good news'. The Evangelists wrote in the conviction that what Jesus had said and done was *the* good news of all time. In Jesus, God had shown himself to be not distant, but near and close at hand. In Jesus, the Kingdom (rule) of God had come down to earth. In Jesus, God's will was being done on earth as it is in heaven.

This belief of theirs colours every page of the four Gospel-writers. They used all the historical material they could find, but also stories, poetry, symbolism, to express what Jesus meant for them. The Gospels are therefore not simple biographies of Jesus, but a profession of faith in Jesus.

# A3 Synoptic Gospels and their write

Mark, symbolized by the winged lion

The first three Gospels (Matthew, Mark and Luke) are called *synoptic*. The word means 'look-alike'. If all three are put into parallel columns, it can easily be seen how alike they are in content and order. Sometimes they are even word-for-word the same. Though they were written in different places and for different readers, they are clearly based on the same collections of sayings and stories about Jesus.

**Mark's Gospel**, written about AD 65.

Mark's Gospel is the earliest. The language is clumsy (try reading it in dialect!) but very vivid. It could be that some of his stories come straight from his friend, Peter, one of Jesus' first followers. Mark's one theme is the mystery of Jesus. '*Who is this?*' (Mark 4:41) He insists that the reader must not answer this question too soon, or too easily. No one can really understand what it means to be Son of God until they see Jesus die on the cross (see Mark 15:39). Are followers of his willing to accept the same fate?

Mark wrote for Christians being persecuted in Rome under the Emperor Claudius.

**Matthew's Gospel**, written about AD 75.

Matthew, symbolized by the divine man

Matthew rewrote Mark's Gospel, imposing his own order on to it. He also interwove it with a great deal of Jesus' teaching not to be found in Mark.

Matthew wrote for the Palestine Jews who had become Christians, and shows Jesus to them as a new Moses who fulfils all that the Jewish sacred writings (the *Old Testament*) had looked forward to. The Jewish style in which he wrote, which is poetic and repetitious, makes his Gospel the most repeatable.

**Luke's Gospel**, written about AD 85.

Like Matthew, Luke based his work on Mark's Gospel, and added to it the teachings of Jesus which Matthew had used, plus a great deal of his own material.

He designed the Gospel as the first of two volumes. The second volume is now called 'The Acts of The Apostles', and tells how he was a friend of Paul, the missionary.

The message of Jesus, as Luke sees it, is not simply a call to martyrdom (as in Mark) or a fulfilment of Jewish hopes (as in Matthew), but a proclamation of consoling news for *all* people to hear.

Luke, symbolized by the winged ox

# A4 More about Luke

Luke was a Greek doctor (Colossians 4:14). He was a friend of Paul and accompanied him on some of his missionary journeys. Neither of them were actual eye-witnesses of Jesus' ministry. Luke was an educated man and wrote in careful Greek. His own compassionate and kindly character shines through the Gospel. He shows more interest in people than in ideas. He had great sympathy for people in trouble. John Drury calls him the 'first humanist'.

Jews and Greeks are very different people. The special character of Greek thought comes out in this Gospel.

### Characteristics of Luke's Gospel

*1. Thoroughness* Luke was concerned to gather all available material before starting his work. A quarter of his Gospel is material not to be found in Mark or Matthew. He assures us it is carefully researched. (See Luke 1:3)

*2. Orderliness* The Greek mind demanded order, everything in its proper place. Luke brought order into the rather disorderly material he collected on his own account. He puts much of this into the framework of a journey to Jerusalem.

*3. Sense of history* Luke wanted to situate Jesus in history, not in mere speculation. He refers to the known political figures of the day to place Jesus in his proper historical context. (Luke 3:1–2)

*4. Sense of moderation* Luke's Jesus is the friend, the good and compassionate man. The very demanding Jesus of Mark is changed by Luke to a calmer figure. Compare Matthew's Jesus who says: *You must be perfect...'* (Matthew 5:48) with Luke's Jesus who says '*You must be merciful...'* (Luke 6:36)

*5. Outward looking* As a Gentile (non-Jew) Luke emphasizes Jesus' interest in the world beyond Judaism. He sees Jesus as the '*Light to reveal* (God's) *will to the Gentiles'*. Throughout the Gospel there is evidence that Luke had great concern (as a doctor?) for the poor, outcasts, sinners and for women.

*6. Spirit of joy* Luke's is the happiest of Gospels. The angel's message in Chapter 2 sums up his Gospel. '*I am here with good news for you, which will bring great joy to all the people.'* (Luke 2:10)

*7. Reservations* Some scholars think that Luke did not write directly to encourage fellow Christians, but to recommend Christianity to the Roman world, and that he idealized things for this purpose.

Misericord from Norwich Cathedral symbolizing Luke

# A5 The land of the Gospels

Palestine is a small country, a strip of land between the sea and the desert. It would easily fit into the South of England.

**The seas and rivers**

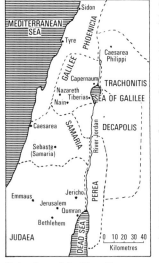

Palestine of the New Testament

To the west lies the Great Sea—the *Mediterranean*. Even with their long coast line, the Jews never had a navy. They thought of the sea as a powerful beast that constantly threatened to overwhelm them.

To the south lies the *Dead Sea*, a most remarkable lake. It is 80 km long and 18 km wide. It lies nearly 400 metres below sea level. The heat of the valley evaporates millions of tons of water every day, leaving the sea rich in minerals. Any fish entering the water from the *River Jordan* die within seconds.

*The Jordan Valley* is part of the Great Rift which stretches from Syria into Africa. In Palestine this rift forms the deepest valley in the world. Trees and bushes are thick near the river; a few yards away the land is desert.

To the north lies the *Sea of Galilee*, which is also part of this rift, 200 metres below sea level. It is a lovely lake and is known as Kinneret (harp-shaped) or the Sea of Tiberias. The town of Tiberias is on the lake shore but Jesus probably never visited it. He was more at home in the fishermen's town of *Capernaum*, on the northern shore. (See Luke 4: 38–9; 7: 1–10; 8: 41–56; 5: 1–11)

Fishing at the Sea of Galilee

## The soil

Compared with the lush countryside of England, the mountainous land of Palestine is harsh and often eroded, especially in the south (Judaea).

This *desert* can be made to bloom if the adequate winter rain is carefully stored, and the hills cut into terraces. In biblical times King Herod channelled winter water so successfully that he could afford a swimming pool in his desert palace on Masada.

Today the desert is again beginning to bloom, this time largely by means of the careful distribution of water by the Israeli Government. Many Israelis work in community farms known as *kibbutzes*, and produce astonishing results from unpromising land.

A few areas of Palestine have always offered more fertile farming:
    the coastal plain (Jaffa oranges);
    parts of the Jordan Valley;
    the Great Plain of southern Galilee

*Olives*, the most important crop, have been grown since biblical times together with grapes, figs, wheat and barley. But citrus fruits, bananas and avocado pears have only been introduced in recent years.

a

d

a Threshing grain
b Camels, 'ships of the desert'
c The Southern Desert
d Sheep being sold
e Terracing for fruit-growing

b

c

e

# A6 The people of the Gospels

The crowds that listened to Jesus were made up of people holding many different religious views. Here are some of the main groups.

### The Pharisees

Pharisees have had a bad name throughout history. This is unfair. They were not all hypocrites. How did they get such a name? Their aim was to become holy by keeping the Law of Moses in exact detail. As laymen they defended the living Word of God, even against the professionals (the priests), who had become too worldly. It is true that some of these Pharisees were Jesus' constant critics. These were the ones for whom *observance of Law* had become an end in itself. But there must have been many Pharisees who welcomed Jesus with open arms.

### The Sadducees

There is evidence in the Acts of the Apostles (4:1, 5:17, etc.) that it was the Sadducees who formed the chief *opposition party* to Jesus and the first Christians.

As the party of priests, landowners and merchants, they were the aristocracy. They stayed in power by collaborating with the Greek and Roman Government. They were conservative in their religious ideas and opposed the Pharisees as too modern.

### The Scribes

In the ancient world, only scholars could read and write. The Jewish writers or Scribes came into prominence 600 years before Christ when with the Temple and monarchy gone, the sacred writings became of great importance. The Scribes collected, copied, edited and interpreted these writings. Jesus complained that they often misinterpreted them.

### The Samaritans

A Samaritan

Samaria had been the capital city of the northern tribes. Destroyed by the Assyrians in 721 BC, most of its inhabitants were exiled and replaced with foreigners from other conquered countries. The mixed race of Samaritans which resulted was never recognized by the Jews, yet they remained faithful to the worship of God and observance of the Law of Moses. They built their own Temple on Mount Gerizim. Jesus shocked his listeners by offering his message of salvation to Samaritans as well as to Jews.

### The Zealots

These were the extremists, the Jewish terrorists active in Palestine during the time of Jesus and after. Their movement was more religious than political, and aimed to rid the country of Roman rule once and for all—even by using violence.

From this unlikely group Jesus chose one of his close followers, Simon the Zealot.

# A7 Life under Roman rule

Glimpses of Ist Century Palestine are still visible in Israel today. There were three distinct ways of life:
- Roman life;
- Jewish life;
- Country life.

## Roman life

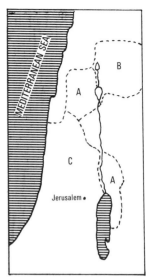

Visitors to the coastal town of *Caesarea* will be surprised as they swim in the bay to see, beneath the waves, columns which once graced the Roman harbour built by Herod the Great. He also erected a palace, theatre, hippodrome and a temple dedicated to the emperor Augustus. Rome made this artificial harbour-town the new capital of Palestine.

At the time of Jesus' birth, Palestine was under Roman rule, as part of the Roman province of Syria. Rome appointed Herod the Great as 'king', and when he died divided his 'kingdom' among his three sons. The map shows their territories.

A. Herod Antipas ruled the north west and south east
B. Philip ruled in the north east
C. Archelaus ruled in the south

Archelaus was a cruel ruler. He was deposed by Rome, and replaced by 'direct rule'. The Roman official who took over was called a 'procurator' or 'governor'. From AD 26 to AD 36 this procurator was *Pontius Pilate* (See Luke 3:1).

Roman soldiers were a familiar sight in Palestine at this time. Their main garrison was at Caesarea-on-Sea. But they also maintained a strong presence in *Jerusalem*, where Herod the Great built the Antonia fortress to overlook the Temple area, a potential trouble spot when feelings ran high against Rome.

The division of Palestine under the Romans

Caesarea

Most visitors to Israel today will visit *Masada*. It is a massive rock near the Dead Sea where the Zealots made a brave last stand against the Romans. Herod had built a superb palace there. When he died in 4 BC it became a Roman garrison. The Zealots captured it, in the rebellion of AD 66. Rather than surrender to the Roman army (who had laid seige to it for 5 years), they committed mass suicide.

*Education*   Roman schools followed the pattern set up in the 5th Century BC in Greece. From six years old boys learned reading, writing and arithmetic. Dance and music were part of religious education, for use in the temple festivals. They aimed to reach a perfect balance between body and mind, so gymnastics and athletics were considered important. Education was completed with public speaking and reasoning. The teachers were often slaves and of very low status.

**Jewish life**

The Jews lived simpler lives than the Romans, although rich Jews (Simon the Pharisee, Luke 7) tried to imitate Roman behaviour. Most Jewish homes were simple, made of branches and mud. Box-like houses of this kind can still be seen today on the hillsides.

Jerusalem, remote in the Judaean hills, was the stronghold of Jewish tradition. Jews streamed to its Temple at the time of their various festivals:

1. Passover
2. Pentecost
3. Tabernacles
4. Atonement or Yom Kippur
5. Dedication or Hannukah
6. Purim

Jerusalem from the Mount of Olives

Masada

Gibeon, a hillside village

There is probably a *synagogue* in your town. This is the place of worship for Jews, when they cannot be in Jerusalem. Jesus attended the synagogue in Nazareth.

From ancient mosaic pictures we know how the 1st Century Jew dressed. Ordinary people, like Jesus, went barefoot or in sandals. They wore a long cotton shirt, a belt and a cloak. At prayer they covered their head with a *tallith* or prayer shawl. Underneath it the males wore a skull cap—as they do today.

Jewish women wore similar clothes, but instead of the tallith they wore a veil. Widows wore black. The young Bedouin girl in the photograph is wearing a dress similar to that worn by Jewish women of Biblical times.

Family life was led in close obedience to the Law of Moses, the *Torah*. There were strict rules about diet. They ate only twice, at midday and evening (the Romans had four meals). Meat, eaten only occasionally, had to be specially killed, with the blood drained out. This was called *kosher* meat. Raw vegetables were spiced with garlic and onions. Olives were the staple diet, with cereals, grapes, nuts, dates and pomegranates. For drink they had milk and wine.

The Jewish mother took a leading role in family life, especially at the festival celebrations in the home. Families cherished the history and rituals of their faith. It was at home that the children learned most about their religious tradition.

Bedouin girl

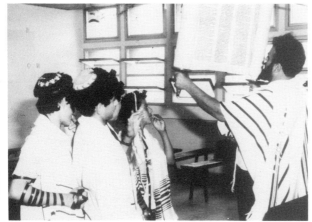

Jewish boys at prayer wearing tallith, tefillin and yarmulka

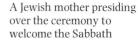

A Jewish mother presiding over the ceremony to welcome the Sabbath

A Jewish boy at his Bar Mitzvah

*Education*

The boys of 1st Century Palestine enjoyed a good education, though they had a very different curriculum from that of Roman schools. Girls received no schooling at all.

Jewish schools regarded their teachers highly. Boys of five or six went to school in the synagogue, where the teaching was totally religious. There was no mathematics, music or physical education. Sitting in a semi-circle on the floor, the young boys learned by a question and answer method. Older boys learned the Law of Moses and discussed theology.

At adolescence the boy received his tallith and took on the adult privileges of the synagogue. This ceremony is called *Bar Mitzvah* (son of the law). It continues to have a great importance for Jews today.

## Country life

Shepherds and fishermen in 1st Century Palestine lived a life not unlike that of shepherds and fishermen in Israel today. They were largely looked down upon by those who lived in towns. Their work in the fields and on the lake made it impossible for them to follow the details of the Jewish Law. This made them outcasts.

Travellers in Israel today will not have to go far to come across a shepherd *leading* his/her sheep. The hard, stony ground in the south makes bad pastureland. Bedouins travel miles, living in tents or caves, to find pasture. In recent times they are being settled in more permanent houses.

The fishermen lived in simple houses in lakeside settlements, like Capernaum. Jesus was to find his first supporters from these country people. As a carpenter, perhaps he mended their boats.

A shepherd leading his flock

Part B

# Luke's Story

# B1 Introduction

Now that we have a background to the 1st Century in Palestine we are ready to look at Luke's Gospel.

Remember that Luke did not write a biography, so we are not going to get a life history of Jesus, from his birth to his death. In fact we really need to look at his life story *back to front*. That is what Luke did. He never knew Jesus, the carpenter and preacher. He only discovered him *after* his death. He was deeply impressed by the effect Jesus had had on his followers. And they claimed that he was 'still alive'. Luke understood what they meant because he too felt his presence and influence. So he wrote his Gospel to share his conviction that the Jesus he was writing about was still alive.

These first followers of Jesus Christ, the first Christians, had something of a problem. Most of them were Jews, like Jesus himself. They believed firmly in only *one* God (unlike the Romans and others).

> *The Lord—and the Lord alone—is our God. Love the Lord your God with all your heart, with all your soul, and with all your strength.*
> Deuteronomy 6:4–5

But they found that whenever they thought of God they also thought about Jesus; and whenever they thought of Jesus, God was in their mind! They became totally convinced that Jesus was very close to God in a special way, but it was difficult to say exactly how.

Jesus had never spoken of himself, but only of God. When he began preaching it was to teach about God's Kingdom. Jesus was a good teacher, he made people sit up and listen. Like most easterners he loved using stories. That is where we will begin.

Everyone loves a story!

# B2 Jesus the preacher – Parables

## The Way In

A man was shown a vision of Hell. He was surprised to see people sitting down at a huge banquet. But no one was eating. They were all struggling to use two-metre-long chopsticks. The man was then shown a vision of Heaven. He was even more surprised because people were sitting down at exactly the same kind of banquet. But this time everyone was eating. They were feeding each other with their two-metre-long chopsticks.

That is a Chinese story.

A story speaks more deeply to people than abstract ideas. A few years ago the 2000 bishops of the Roman Catholic Church met together to reconsider all the beliefs of that church. The meeting was called the Second Vatican Council. It lasted three years. Someone asked an Indian bishop what his people thought of the Council. *'Nothing at all,'* he said, *'because they don't understand what the Council is talking about.'* 'Well, what would they understand?' he was asked. And with a sigh the Indian bishop said, *'Oh, if only the Council would tell us a story.'*

Great religous leaders have often used stories to teach their followers.

Here is a Dervish story told by Sheikh Nasir el-Din Shah.

*A worried man promised on oath that if his problems were solved he would sell his house and give all the money away to the poor. The time came when he realized that he must do what he promised. But he did not want to give away so much money. So he thought of a way out. He put the house on sale at one silver piece. Included with the house, however was a cat. The price he asked for this animal was ten thousand pieces of silver. The house and cat were sold. The man gave the single piece of silver to the poor, and put the ten thousand into his own pocket.*

Here is a Jewish story.

*The Rabbi of Witkowo, out walking with his son, told him to give a penny to a blind beggar. The boy did so and ran back to his father. 'But why didn't you raise your hat?' asked his father. 'He wouldn't have seen me,' said the boy, 'because he is blind.' 'And how do you know that he is not an imposter?' replied the Rabbi, 'Go and raise your hat to him.'*

This is a story Jesus told.

*Two men owed a moneylender money. One owed him £500; the other £50. They hadn't a penny in the world; so the moneylender crossed their debts out. Which of the two men would most want to say 'Thank you' to him?*

as modernised by A. T. Dale, *New World* (O.U.P., 1967)

## Main Issues

The disciples of Jesus called his stories *parables*. The word means 'to compare like with like'. It was a well-understood teaching method of the Jewish rabbis or teachers, so the parables of Jesus are similar to those of his Jewish teachers.

It is in Luke's Gospel that we find the best-known of the stories people said Jesus told. And it is in these stories that Jesus described what God was like, and what his rule over men was like. The Gospels call this the Kingdom of God.

Read Luke 4:14–20. It describes the beginning of Jesus' preaching life. From then on, Jesus taught the people in the towns and villages. He told them many stories. When, for example, complaints were made that Jesus welcomed sinners, he didn't start explaining in abstract terms about God's attitude of forgiveness and welcome. He told stories about the joy of a shepherd who finds a sheep of his that had strayed, and the joy of a woman who finds a coin she had lost.

Jesus, through his parables, was challenging the ideas of his contemporaries about the true nature of the Kingdom for which they were waiting:

> The Kingdom is not some earth-shaking event to come in the future.
> The Kingdom is here and now.
> The Kingdom is not reserved for a chosen few.
> The Kingdom is for anyone who will accept it.

We misread the parables if we treat them as general moral exhortations (Be good, be just, be honest, etc). Parables are questions and they contain a sort of surprise twist which upsets the normal order of things. These stories always give us a fresh vision of God whose ways, says Jesus, *are* different from ours. Jesus wanted to challenge the people's superficial notions about God. And he did it, sometimes gently, sometimes harshly and sometimes tongue-in-cheek.

### Parables and the Kingdom

The parables were all to do with God's Way (the Kingdom of God). Their purpose was to explain what God's Way (Kingdom) is like, and what it is not like. Luke has thirty-five parables telling us what God's Way is like.

> *The Kingdom of God is like this. A woman takes some yeast and mixes it with forty litres of flour until the whole batch of dough rises.*
>
> Luke 13:20–21

And Luke has twenty-two parables or sayings telling us what those unprepared for the Kingdom are like.

> *Salt is good, but if it loses its saltiness, there is no way to make it salty again. It is no good for the soil or for the manure heap; it is thrown away.*
>
> Luke 14:34–35

The woman of the lost coin?

| What the Kingdom of God is like | | What those unprepared for the Kingdom are like | |
|---|---|---|---|
| | Luke | | Luke |
| Doctor healing the sick | 5:31 | Patched garment | 5:36 |
| Bridegroom and his guests | 5:34 | Old wineskins | 5:37 |
| *New wine | 5:37 | Blind leading the blind | 6:39 |
| Generous measure | 6:38, 8:18, 19:26 | Unseen log | 6:41 |
| House built on rock | 6:47 | Bad fruit tree | 6:43 |
| Abundant harvest | 8:5 | House built on sand | 6:49 |
| Lamp on a lampstand | 8:16, 11:33 | Peevish children | 7:31 |
| *Good Samaritan | 10:30 | Lamp under a bowl | 8:16, *11:33 |
| *Importunate friend (nagging) | 11:5 | Empty house | 11:24 |
| *Importunate widow (nagging) | 18:1 | Bad eye | 11:34 |
| Hungry child fed | 11:11 | *Rich fool | 12:16 |
| Victory over divided Kingdom | 11:17 | Careless servant | 12:42 |
| Victory over strong man | 11:21 | Bad weather forecasters | 12:54 |
| Treasure kept safe | 12:33 | Debtor | 12:57 |
| Bridegroom at night | 12:35 | *Unfruitful fig tree | 13:6 |
| Thief at night | 12:39 | *Locked out | 13:25 |
| Mustard tree | 13:18 | Savourless salt | 14:34 |
| Leavened loaf | 13:20 | Slave of two masters | 16:13 |
| Narrow door | 13:24 | *Rich miser | 16:19 |
| *Last place | 14:7 | *Proud Pharisee | 18:9 |
| *Poor guests | 14:12 | *Murderous vinedressers | 20:9 |
| Great feast | 14:16 | | |
| *Tower builder | 14:28 | | |
| *King going to war | 14:31 | | |
| Lost sheep found | 15:4 | | |
| *Lost coin found | 15:8 | | |
| *Lost son found | 15:11 | | |
| *Ruthless manager | 16:1 | | |
| One taken one left | 17:34 | | |
| Vultures and carcase | 17:37 | | |
| Money in trust | 19:12 | | |
| Flowering fig tree | 21:29 | (*parables only found in Luke) | |

## Background to the Parables

It is very important with any parable to look at the background in which it was told. It must always be related to the original situation. It can be assumed that the hearers of Jesus were familiar with the Old Testament and hence recognized at once the images Jesus used. It is all too easy to look for clues to its interpretation in ideas that developed much later, through the experience of the early church.

Let us take a look at two of the parables in more detail.

*Prodigal Son* (Lost Son)   Luke 15:11–32
The boy had done an enormous injustice to his father. It was as though he said to his father, 'I wish you were dead.' The parable, however, is about the father. He is the one who is prodigal, wasteful. He wastes his love and forgiveness on the boy with *no* conditions attached. He looks for him. He kisses him. He celebrates with him. Now why does the story shock the crowd?

1. Because they are being told that God shows no distinction between those who have and those who have not obeyed the Law.

> He makes his sun shine on good and bad alike,
> His gentle rain falls on saints and sinners.
>                     from H. J. Richards *The Gospel in Song* (Mayhew, 1983)

It seems totally unjust. God is more lavish than we ever want to be.

2. Because the Old Testament had made them accustomed to identifying themselves with the younger son. Isaac and Jacob were the younger sons, blessed by God (See Genesis, Chapters 16–21 and Chapter 25). Here Jesus is identifying his audience with the disgruntled elder son. There are others, he is saying, latecomers to the Good News, over whom God really rejoices.

It is easy to see how shocked the crowd must have been at this story, and they would have been just as outraged at the story of the Good Samaritan.

*Good Samaritan*   Luke 10:29–37

It is necessary to understand what Jesus' contemporaries thought of priests, Levites and Samaritans to get the thrust of this story (See page 8).

To make it more understandable to us, teachers today have often retold this famous parable in a modern setting. For example, a Catholic priest in Belfast read the following parable to his congregation.

> *A Roman Catholic woman from the Falls Road, Belfast was out shopping and got caught in an exchange of gunfire. She was hit and lay in the road injured.*
>
> *An I.R.A. sympathiser passed by. He did not stop because he didn't want to get involved.*
>
> *A nun was hurrying along the road. She didn't stop to see what was the matter because she didn't want to be late for her prayers.*
>
> *Then a Protestant terrorist drove down the road. He saw the woman lying in a pool of blood. He stopped the car, ran over and lifted her into the car. He drove her to the hospital as fast as he could.*
>
> *Which one of these three, do you think, acted in the most godly manner?*

The Catholic congregation listening to this would be very disturbed.

## Further Issues

Understanding and interpreting the gospel parables is not a straightforward exercise. There are problems. The parable of the *Sower* illustrates this (Luke 8:5–15).

Luke, with Matthew and Mark, tells the story of the Sower and then says that the disciples asked Jesus what this parable meant. Now why did Jesus say, according to the Evangelists, that he used parables to make it impossible for some people to understand?

> *His disciples asked Jesus what this parable meant and he answered, 'The knowledge of the secrets of the Kingdom of God has been given to you, but to the rest it comes by means of parables, so that they may look but not see, and listen and not understand.'*
>                                   (Luke 8:9–10)

The other pages of the Gospels do *not* give us the impression of a Jesus who deliberately makes his teaching unintelligible. It seems more likely that this strange text reflects the thinking of the early church. The evangelists and their companions must have asked themselves just why so many of Jesus' contemporaries didn't follow him. This text could be their attempt to solve the problem.

Luke continues, in Chapter 8, to give an explanation by Jesus of the parable. Now it is most unlikely that Jesus would spell out the detailed meaning of the parable. This decoding of a story, phrase by phrase, is treating the story as an *allegory*. This was utterly foreign to Jewish thought. But it was very common in the Greek world, and we know that the early church was quickly influenced by the Greek world.

It is probably nearer the truth to suggest that the parable of the Sower was a very optimistic comment by Jesus on the fact that farmers produce wonderful harvests even though some of the seed gets lost. Farmers never give up sowing because what they get from the harvest is always greater than what they have given away in sowing.

The early church, influenced by the Greek world, treated many of the parables as allegories and they went into great detail 'explaining' them. One famous example is Augustine's interpretation of the parable of the Good Samaritan. It begins:

> *A certain man went down from Jerusalem to Jericho. Adam himself is meant; Jerusalem is the heavenly city of peace from whose blessedness Adam fell; Jericho means the moon, and signifies our mortality, because it is born, waxes, wanes and dies. Thieves are the devil and his angels. Who stripped him, namely of his immortality; and beat him, by persuading him to sin; . . .*
>
> quoted by C. H. Dodd *The Parables of the Kingdom* (Nisbet, 1935)

---

Whatever Jesus meant when he first told his parables, he *was* speaking poetry. And there is no right or wrong way of interpreting poetry.

---

## A   Quick answers on the text.

1.   Before the telling of the parable of the Good Samaritan, who asked Jesus what he should do to inherit eternal life?

2.   For whose benefit especially did Jesus tell the story of the two debtors?

3.   What was the complaint which Luke said prompted Jesus to tell the parables of the Lost Sheep, the Lost Coin and the Lost Son?

4.   Give *two* of the reasons which the guests gave for not attending the great banquet in the parable.

5.   Which parable concludes with the words, '*And so I say to you, ask, and you will receive; seek, and you will find; knock, and the door will be opened to you.*'

6.   '*People who are well do not need a doctor, but only those who are sick.*' Jesus interprets this parable in the next sentence. What is it?

7.   The parable in question 6, above, would appeal very much to Luke. Why?

8.   In the parables about hospitality what kind of guests does Jesus advise his listeners to invite.

9.   In the parable of the Rich Man and Lazarus, who said: '*your brothers have Moses and the Prophets to warn them.*'?

10.   According to Luke, who asked Jesus to explain the meaning of the parable of the Sower?

## B   Longer answers

1.   Write a paragraph to describe what a parable is.

2.   Rewrite one of the parables putting it into a modern setting.

3.   In the parable of the Pharisee and Publican (tax-collector), Jesus taught about prayer.
    (a) Explain why Jesus chose a Pharisee and a tax-collector for the parable.
    (b) What did Jesus say about their prayer?
    (c) Name another parable about prayer.

4.   Retell in your own words the parable of the Gold Coins (Luke 19:11ff) (money in trust).

5.   Make a list of the parables which are found only in Luke.

## C   Essays

1.   Refer to the parables of the Lost (Sheep, Coin, Son) to show what Jesus taught about God's attitude to sinful people.

2.   Tell in your own words the parable of the Wicked Tenants. Why is it usually regarded as an allegory? Describe another parable in the Gospel which is treated as an allegory.

3.   Describe in detail the parable of the Good Samaritan. Do you think it is a relevant story for today?

4.   Referring to many of the parables in the list on page 17, write an essay describing the Kingdom of God as Jesus saw it.

## D   For individuals and groups to do

1.   Choose a parable and try to turn it into an allegory.

2.   Prepare a slide programme (with music and readings) to illustrate the parables.

3.   Find out some more stories from other religious traditions. Make a group book of *Great Stories*. Artists in the group could illustrate it.

4.   Write a parable to accompany the picture below.

# B3 The infancy story

## The Way In

Jesus used stories in his teaching. Luke used stories too, stories to tell people that Jesus was a unique person. Perhaps the most familiar story about Jesus is the Christmas story. People are reminded of it year after year. Children act out nativity plays, choirs sing carols and families put crib-figures by the Christmas tree.

> *Silent night, holy night,*
> *all is calm, all is bright,*
> *round yon virgin mother and child;*
> *holy infant so tender and mild;*
> *sleep in heavenly peace,*
> *sleep in heavenly peace.*
>
> *Silent night, holy night,*
> *Shepherds quake at the sight,*
> *glories stream from heaven afar,*
> *heavenly hosts sing alleluia:*
> *Christ, the Saviour is born,*
> *Christ, the Saviour is born.*
>
> Joseph Mohr (1792–1848) tr. J. Young

Christmas cards appear in the shops around September. Some have non-religious themes but many continue to portray a part of the Christmas story. Luke and Matthew are the two Gospel writers who give us stories about the birth and childhood of Jesus. But the two accounts are very different.

The Annunciation, Wells
Cathedral

The well-known carol 'Silent Night' and the Wells Cathedral relief of
the angel meeting Mary were inspired by Luke's story. Matthew's story
does not contain these details. Luke describes Mary's amazement at the
announcement by an angel that she is to have a child. He describes a
visit Mary makes to her cousin Elizabeth who is also pregnant. He
describes the birth of Jesus in poverty at Bethlehem, and the visit of the
shepherds. He describes how Joseph and Mary dedicated the child to God
in the Temple. Then he ends his infancy narrative with a strange story
of the boy Jesus being lost, and found in the Temple.

Roman Catholics have for centuries had a tradition of meditating on
these stories. They finger a set of beads, called a *rosary*, as they think
about the *Five Joyful Mysteries* recorded in Luke, Chapters 1 and 2.
These Five Mysteries are:

    The Annunciation
    The Visitation
    The Nativity
    The Presentation
    The Finding in the Temple.

Notice how Luke includes so many women in his infancy story.
Matthew's account is very different. It is only Matthew who describes
the visit of the Wise Men and the massacre of baby boys which led to
Joseph taking his family into Egypt.

Why did only two of the New Testament writers tell stories of the
childhood of Jesus? Did they have special information? Were they
recording something that they knew really happened? Were there really
angels, wise men and shepherds at Bethlehem? Was Jesus really born
in an animals' stable? What happened 2000 years ago?

We will take a closer look at the text to see if we can answer some of
these questions.

A rosary

# Main Issues

Read Chapters 1 and 2 of the Gospel.

### The Angel stories

The first thing to notice is that we are reading a double story. There are two births, unlikely ones at that, the birth of John the Baptist and the birth of Jesus. Both are announced by the angel. Both are described. This is followed in each case by the story of the children's circumcision, naming and early life. Both boys are destined to be great.

Luke wants to make sure we don't miss this parallelism because he keeps using similar phrases in describing the two series of events. Read the two chapters with your eye on the following points:

| The Angel visits Zechariah | The Angel visits Mary |
|---|---|
| Zechariah and Elizabeth | Joseph and Mary |
| Enter the Angel Gabriel | Enter the Angel Gabriel |
| Zechariah was alarmed and afraid | Mary was deeply troubled |
| 'Don't be afraid' | 'Don't be afraid' |
| Elizabeth is to bear a son | Mary is to bear a son |
| 'You are to name him John' | 'You will name him Jesus' |
| 'He will be a great man' | 'He will be great' |
| His task is described | His task is described |
| How shall I know if this is so?' | 'How then, can this be?' |
| A sign is given | A sign is given |

Luke concludes the two stories with almost the same words: '(John) grew and developed in body and spirit.' (Luke 1:80) and 'Jesus grew both in body and wisdom.' (Luke 2:52)

We have to conclude from this that Luke is writing in a very careful, artistic way. He wants symmetry and harmony in his writing. He wants his readers to appreciate how alike these two men were, John the Baptist and Jesus. And this is to prepare them for John's own declaration that, in fact, Jesus towers above him. At the start of the main part of Luke's Gospel John the Baptist is going to say: 'Someone is coming who is much greater than I am.' (Luke 3:16)

### Where did the story come from?

We are at a great disadvantage when we read Luke, because we don't know the Old Testament inside out. His first readers would have said: 'Ah, Luke is sending us back to the Samuel story.'

1 Samuel begins with the story of a mother who is childless. She has an assurance from heaven that she will give birth. She has a son whom she presents in the Temple. She sings a song of praise to God for his power and graciousness. The story concludes with the young Samuel continuing 'to grow and to gain favour both with the Lord and with men.' (1 Samuel 2:26).

There are other birth stories like this in the Old Testament. Take a look at the joy of Abraham and Sarah when Isaac was born (Genesis 21), or look at the birth of Samson (Judges 13).

The message of all these stories is that true leadership of mankind is always a creation of God. And Luke is anxious to point out that it is Jesus who is the ultimate 'God-send'.

## Mary's song

Read again Luke 1:46–56. Mary's song has become one of the great hymns of the Christian church. It is known as the *Magnificat* and it is sung in parish churches and cathedrals at Evensong. Roman Catholic monks and nuns sing it daily in their prayer called Vespers. Down the ages great musicians have set it to music.

> *The Lord has filled my heart with joy;*
> *how happy I am because of what he has done...*
> *how joyful I am because God has helped me!*
>
> *No one is holy like the Lord;*
> *there is none like him...*
> *The bows of strong soldiers are broken,*
> *but the weak grow strong...*
>
> *He makes some men poor and others rich;*
> *he humbles some and makes others great.*
> *He lifts the poor from the dust*
> *and raises the needy from their misery.*
> *He makes them companions of princes*
> *and puts them in places of honour...*
>
> *The Lord will give power to his king,*
> *he will make his chosen king victorious.*

The prayer you have just read is *not* Mary's prayer. But notice how similar it is. This one is the prayer of Hannah, Samuel's mother (See again 1 Samuel 1 and 2). Compare the two songs. Perhaps Mary sang the song of Hannah that she knew so well in order to express her own joy. Or perhaps Luke put the words into Mary's mouth because they are so appropriate.

It has often been noted that the hymn is revolutionary in its content. It doesn't settle for a nice, comfortable way of life. Someone once said 'the *Magnificat* is the most revolutionary document in the world,' that is it is meant to cause an upheaval.

William Barclay in *The Daily Study Bible, The Gospel of Luke* examines the revolutionary aspect of this prayer. It is worth a closer look. He concludes the section: *There is a loveliness in the* Magnificat *but in this loveliness there is dynamite. Christianity begets a revolution in each man and revolution in the world.*

The Orthodox tradition is that Mary received the angel's message while drawing water from the Nazareth well

## Two Other Songs

As we would expect, from what we have already seen of parallelism in Luke's infancy story, there is a hymn sung in praise of God at the birth of John the Baptist. This time, however, it is the father Zechariah, who sings God's praise. The prayer is known as the *Benedictus* and it is sung at the church's morning prayer (Luke 1:68–79).

A third hymn from these chapters of Luke (Luke 2:29) is the prayer of Simeon. This song is known as the *Nunc Dimittis* and is sung at the church's evening prayer.

These songs are often called *canticles*.

Singing God's praises

## Further Issues

Luke doesn't quote directly from the Old Testament and this makes it difficult for us to recognize how dependent on the Old Testament he really was for his infancy story. Here is just an indication of how deeply Luke had meditated on the Hebrew Scriptures, which Christians call their Old Testament.

There are great *themes* which run through the Old Testament and many of these main themes Luke introduces in the stories of Jesus' birth.

### 1. Redemption
Zechariah's prayer, for example, echoes Daniel's pleading with God to send redemption to his people. Compare Luke 1:8–11, 19 and Daniel 9:20–25.

Jesus, says Luke, is the redemption yearned for by the Old Testament.

### 2. Day of the Lord
John the Baptist is described as Elijah the Prophet. Elijah was to come before the Day of the Lord (Malachi 4:5–6).

Jesus, says Luke, brings the Day of the Lord.

### 3. The coming of God
Many Old Testament texts speak of the joy there will be when God comes (Zechariah 9:9; Joel 2:21, 23; Zephaniah 3:14–17).

The greeting of the angel to Mary is in the same vein. Jesus, says Luke, makes God in our midst a reality.

### 4. The presence of God
In the books of Exodus and Numbers God was present to his people in their desert journey. The cloud was the symbol of his presence and it was said to 'cover with its shadow' the people on their journey (Exodus 24:16–17, and 40:34; Numbers 9:15–22).

Mary, says Luke, was covered with God's shadow and he was present in her womb.

*The 2nd Century Ark on wheels, Capernaum Synagogue*

### 5.  *Ark of the Covenant*

The joyful description of Mary's visit to Elizabeth is based on the story of David dancing before the Ark of the Covenant (2 Samuel 6: 5, 14). David took the Ark to the house of Obed Edom and *'it stayed there three months'* (2 Samuel 6: 11).

*'Mary stayed about three months with Elizabeth'* (Luke 1: 56). Mary, says Luke, is the Ark of the Covenant 'housing' the presence of God in her womb.

### 6.  *Poverty*

In the latter part of the Old Testament, poverty is seen as the necessary condition for knowing God. The poor, called *anawim,* have nothing to rely upon but God. Hannah is one of the *anawim,* and in her song (1 Samuel 2: 8) she exults in her poverty which God has noticed.

Mary, says Luke, is blessed because of her poverty.

> *My heart praises the Lord . . .*
> *for he has remembered me, his lowly servant! . . .*
> *He has brought down mighty kings from their thrones*
> *and lifted up the lowly.*
>
> Luke 1:46, 48, 52

This theme is a favourite one for Luke. He will return to it again and again. The poor baby in a stable, recognized by poor people, is already a summary of the whole of Luke's Gospel. It says it all. (See pages 86–90.)

### 7.  *Jerusalem*

Jerusalem is very important to Luke. Half of his Gospel is set on one long journey to Jerusalem. He echoes this idea in the infancy story. The climax of his story is also a journey which finishes in Jerusalem. It is the story of the young boy Jesus making his *bar-mitzvah* journey to the Temple in Jerusalem. *'Didn't you know that I had to be in my Father's house?'* he asks (Luke 2:49).

The Temple theme which runs through the Old Testament is being echoed here too. Already Luke has hinted at the importance of the Temple in the Song of Zechariah, when he links verses 76–78 in Chapter 1 to Malachi 3:1. *'I will send my messenger to prepare the way for me. Then the Lord you are looking for will suddenly come to his Temple.'*

### 8.  *Rome*

Rome too is important for Luke. So it is not surprising that he brings Rome into his first chapters. The Gospel of Jesus is for everyone. Bethlehem, said Matthew, is the birthplace of Jesus because he is second David. Bethlehem, says Luke, is the birthplace of Jesus because Rome decreed it so.

## The Virgin Birth

Read again Luke 1:26–38. This text brings us up against one of the most challenging of Christian beliefs, the birth of Jesus from a virgin mother. For centuries most Christians have taken the words of Luke at face value. They believe that Jesus was born of Mary without having a human father. But some Christians, especially today, read the stories as poetry. We will look at both viewpoints.

Mary
and
Jesus

*The traditional view*
This is the view that Luke meant exactly what he said—that Mary remained a virgin before, during and after the birth of Jesus. Jesus had no human father. Joseph was only his foster father.

It is the Roman Catholic church which has presented this view of Mary's virginity most persistently. The early creeds and councils of the church spoke of Mary as a 'virgin'. But it was not for several hundred years that a church council (Constantinople II in AD 553) made this word into a solemn doctrine, by proclaiming that Mary always remained literally a virgin.

This interpretation of Mary's virginity is based on the following assumptions:
1. Luke 1:26–38 and Matthew 1:18–25 are to be read literally. The texts mean what they say, that Jesus had no human father.
2. Jesus is divine, the Son of God. Being a unique person it is natural to presume that his birth was also unique, even biologically.

This traditional view fits in well with an old belief that Luke was a personal friend of Mary. Besides being a doctor he was an artist, who painted her portrait and shared her intimate memories. How else could he have known how Mary gave birth to Jesus?

*The other view*
Many Christians today, including theologians (some, Roman Catholic) find it more helpful to interpret Mary's virginity in a different way. A literal virginity of Mary is not needed in their understanding of the text. Luke, they believe, is using a carefully worked out and poetic story in order to emphasize the uniqueness of Jesus. To support this view they make the following observations:
1. The list of names in Luke and Matthew (Luke 3:23–38, Matthew 1:1–17) trace the genealogy of Jesus through Joseph. Why, if Joseph wasn't his real father?
2. Jesus is known as Joseph's son throughout the gospels. Even Mary says '*your father and I*' (Luke 2:48) and she means Joseph.
3. There is no other reference to the virgin birth in the rest of the New Testament.
4. The Luke story is so clearly based on Old Testament, miraculous birth stories. They themselves were written in a well-known, literary poetic form, where all births are regarded as the gift of God. There is, for example, a story in the Apocrypha where the mother of the Maccabee martyrs speaks of the birth of her children: '*I do not know how you appeared in my womb; it was not I who endowed you with breath and life . . . . It is the creator of the world, ordaining the process of man's birth*' (2 Maccabees 7:22–23).

5. Luke was interested in the themes which ran through the Old Testament (See page 25). The theme of poverty was of special interest to him and the theme of virginity was very close to this. In Old Testament thought virginity is a state of desolation. It spells failure, misery, emptiness. Luke needed a virgin in his story because only then could God be seen to transform the emptiness into fullness.

It is suggested that in his birth stories Luke is already pointing to the emptiness of the tomb which, through the resurrection, is transformed into fullness of life.

In this non-literal view of the meaning of virgin birth some Christians think that the biological fact is not important. What really happened to Mary? Who knows? It may well have been the ordinary, human event of a young couple having a baby. Luke is saying 'look deeper'. In the light of all that this baby eventually proved to be, his birth was a decisive moment in history. For this child was eventually going to show himself to be a son of God in a unique way and the earth could never be the same again.

A children's nativity play

For some Christians it is important to believe that Mary was literally always a virgin. It helps them to have faith in a God who can do the impossible.

For other Christians it is important to believe that Mary was not literally a virgin. They can't accept a God who makes strange interventions into history, because it makes him less credible. These Christians are helped by faith in a God whom they see most clearly in an utterly human Jesus.

**What do we conclude about the infancy narrative?**

The Christmas story in Luke is Chapter 1 and 2 of the Gospel. It comes at the beginning but it was, in fact, added to the rest of the story later. Luke was convinced that all God's plans had been fulfilled in the death and resurrection of Jesus. He wanted to show that they were already fulfilled when Jesus was born, even when he was conceived in the womb. He added the stories to make that clear.

Luke was writing for adults. We mustn't think that these are only nice little stories for children. But Luke was not writing a history book about Jesus. The stories do not tell us *how* and *where* and *when* Jesus was born and grew up, but they tell us *who* Jesus is.

Luke was writing hundreds of years ago, in the Middle East. How can we ever know exactly what happened so long ago? But Luke is not telling us a 'tall' story. He is telling us a very deep one. He uses a literary form unlike any we use today in Western Europe. His story is a meditation on all the Old Testament themes. He took many of the Old Testament texts and rewrote them to make them apply to Jesus, because he saw Jesus as the completion of all those themes. We call his literary form of writing *midrash*.

## A Quick answers on the text

1. In which town was Jesus brought up?
2. Who was Simeon?
3. Who were the parents of John the Baptist?
4. To whom was Mary promised in marriage?
5. Who was Anna?
6. Name the Roman emperor at the time of Jesus' birth.
7. Where did Jesus' parents take him when he was 12 years old?
8. Who said, '*My heart praises the Lord; My soul is glad because of God my Saviour*'?
9. Who does Luke say visited Jesus when he was lying in a manger?
10. Name the two occasions in Luke's infancy story when the Angel Gabriel is mentioned.
11. Which town is 'David's town'?
12. What is *midrash*?

## B Longer answers

1. Put the Song of Hannah and Mary's song side by side, so that you can see which line echoes which.
2. *His mother said to him, 'My son, why have you done this to us? Your father and I have been terribly worried trying to find you!'* (Luke 2:48)
What had caused this worry? Comment on Jesus' reply.
3. What was the Passover Festival in Jerusalem that Jesus attended with his parents?
4. How many songs does Luke quote in his infancy narrative? Who sung or said them?
5. Describe in your own words the meeting between Mary and her cousin, Elizabeth.

## C Essays

1. What did Luke write about the birth and boyhood of Jesus to show that there was something unique about him?
2. What does Luke tell us about (a) the visit of the angel Gabriel to Mary and (b) the visit of Mary to Elizabeth? Comment on any one point which you find interesting in these stories.
3. Describe in your own words the visit of Jesus to Jerusalem at the age of twelve. Comment on any *two* points you find interesting.
4. Retell the stories of (a) Gabriel's visit to Mary and (b) the shepherds' visit to Mary and Joseph. Why do these stories present some difficulties for the modern reader?
5. In what way is Mary's song, the *Magnificat*, a revolutionary song? Where in today's world might a persecuted people find it appropriate?

## D For individuals and groups to do

1. Write your own Christmas carol.
2. Design a modern Christmas card or make a Christmas collage.
3. Get the whole class/group to make a collection of Christmas cards. Put them on display and find their gospel references (if any). Hold a discussion about them.
4. If you are interested in music either: (a) learn a version of the *Magnificat* to sing to your group, or (b) write your own musical version.
5. Compose a ten-minute slide and music programme for the Christmas season.

# B4 Jesus the wonderworker – Mirac

**The Way In**

## Mother's joy at 'miracle'

A boy aged two, sent to Britain from the Irish Republic in a last attempt to save his life, left hospital yesterday after what his mother called 'a miracle' cure.

Anthony Hurley, from Cork, had a massive spinal tumour and was given six months to live. He should now lead a normal life.

Doctors in the republic said the tumour was inoperable so the boy's parents wrote to the Queen's Medical Centre, Nottingham. Their letter—addressed to 'A Doctor'—reached Mr John Firth, a leading neurosurgeon. The tumour was found to be non-malignant.

"The people involved were sent from heaven, I'm sure of that", the child's mother, Mrs Jacqueline Hurley, said.

Mrs Hurley is quite sure that miracles happen today. What would you call a *miracle*? A number of people were asked that question recently. Here are their replies.

*In the recent gales an enormous tree fell onto a school pre-fab building. It wrecked the whole building but all the 30 girls inside the classroom were completely unhurt. That surely was a miracle.*

Stephen, university student

*If the Kremlin suddenly announced it would unilaterally get rid of its nuclear weapons.*

Tony, a social worker

*The birth of a baby.*

Mary-Anne, 19-year-old student

*I was a hospital chaplain. On four occasions I was present when a doctor diagnosed terminal illness. On each occasion the nursing sister whispered, 'Not if I can help it.' I watched her will these patients back to life. Her dedication, skill, care and willpower proved the doctors wrong. All four lived. Those were miracles of healing.*

Former hospital chaplain

*More than three years ago I had to leave my boy-friend in South America while I came to study in England. Yesterday I had a phone call to tell me he had arrived in Europe. It is a miracle.*

Claudia, young Colombian student

*We had a bill for £55 which we simply couldn't pay. We prayed about it together. The very next day a totally unexpected letter arrived in which there was a cheque for exactly £55. It was miraculous.*

Young couple

*I gave a music teacher the simple melody line of a song I wanted to check. He looked at it and immediately played it on the piano with full accompaniment. To me that was miraculous.*

Bert, an amateur songwriter

*We needed a teacher for Religious Studies at our school—and at very short notice. As our community was going on a pilgrimage to the shrine at Walsingham we all decided to pray for this intention. One sister got into conversation with one of the helpers there, telling her of our intention. To the sister's amazement the helper told her she was a teacher of Religious Studies, just returned from voluntary work in Fiji, and anxious for a job. The meeting was a miracle.*

Sister Mary, headmistress

Would you have called all these events 'miracles'? Many people would say that they are all quite easy to explain in natural terms and therefore there is *nothing miraculous* about them. For these people a miracle is 'an event or action which violates the laws of nature'. It is something which causes a scientist or a doctor to say: 'But that simply can't happen.'

It is interesting that no one in the survey described that kind of miracle. For each of them, their miracle was an event which filled them with wonder and awe. As one of them said: 'a miracle is something which sends a shiver up my spine.'

Mary-Anne's miracle is such an ordinary human event that it happens thousands of times a day! Sister Mary's miracle could just have been a chance meeting, and the young couple's 'windfall' a mere coincidence. Even the hospital chaplain's healings can be understood in today's medical world.

So where is the miraculous? Does it lie in the eyes of the beholder?

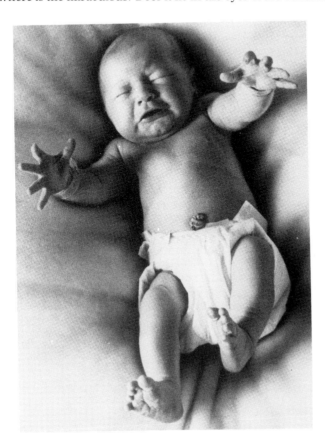

## Main Issues

What exactly were the miracles of Jesus? Scholars have argued long over that question. Miracle stories were common in the Old Testament but also in the ancient Near East outside the Old Testament, and in the Mediterranean world outside the New Testament. Jesus wasn't alone in working miracles.

Miracle stories appear in all religious traditions—Hindu, Buddhist, Islamic and Christian—from the earliest times down to the present day.

One of the most striking things about the story of Jesus is that his public ministry was accompanied, all the way through, by miracles. Luke tells us, in the Acts of the Apostles, that the disciples began their preaching by reminding the crowds of this well-known fact:

> *Jesus of Nazareth was a man whose divine authority was clearly proven to you all by the miracles and wonders which God performed through him.*

> Acts 2:22

When this preaching was put into writing by the gospel writers, miracles were given the same prominence. But what makes it difficult to know what Jesus actually did is the fact that the four evangelists themselves played an important part in the miracle stories they told.

They selected the stories which would serve their purpose. They arranged them and sometimes retold them with further details to fit their own wider concerns. A miracle story told by Mark, for example, may be retold by Luke with quite a different emphasis.

Luke tells us that Jesus announced his ministry in Nazareth. He proclaimed his *Manifesto* in the words of Isaiah.

> *The Spirit of the Lord is upon me,*
> *because he has chosen me to bring good news to the poor.*
> *He has sent me to proclaim liberty to captives*
> *and recovery of sight to the blind;*
> *to set free the oppressed*
> *and announce that the time has come*
> *when the Lord will save his people.*

> Isaiah 61:1–2; Luke 4:18–19

This text, said Jesus, is now fulfilled. The great day is here. God's Kingdom is come. Luke selects stories about Jesus to show that this was so. Every miracle story is a sign that the Kingdom had come in Jesus.

Luke doesn't seem to find anything awesome and mysterious about the miracles. They are simply what would be expected from someone who was filled with the *Spirit of God*. With the Spirit of God so fully in him the Kingdom of God had come amongst people, and this had set people free. The miracle stories for Luke are illustrations that people were set free by the love and compassion of this travelling preacher, this down-to-earth man.

Jesus healing the blind, from a
17th Century Ethiopian painting

## The miracles recorded by Luke

The miracles fall naturally into four groups. For Luke Jesus sets people free:

(a) *From the power of the Devil*

| Luke | 4:33 | A man with an evil spirit |
|---|---|---|
| | 4:41 | Demons in many people |
| | 6:18 | Those troubled by evil spirits |
| | 8:26 | A man with demons in him |
| | 9:37 | A boy with an evil spirit |
| | 11:14 | A possessed man who could not talk |

(b) *From all that prevents people living fully:*

| Luke | 4:38 | Simon's mother-in-law who was sick |
|---|---|---|
| | 4:40 | Sick friends |
| | 5:12 | A man with a dreaded skin disease |
| | 5:18 | A paralysed man |
| | 6:6 | A man with a paralysed hand |
| | 6:19 | Many diseases |
| | 7:2 | A Roman officer's servant |
| | 7:21 | Many diseases, including blindness |
| | 8:43 | A woman with severe bleeding |
| | 13:11 | A crippled woman* |
| | 14:2 | A sick man* |
| | 17:12 | Ten men with skin disease (lepers)* |
| | 18:35 | A blind beggar |
| | 22:50 | The High Priest's slave* |

(c) *From a world in disharmony with man*

| Luke | 5:4 | The catch of fish |
|---|---|---|
| | 8:22 | Calming a storm at sea |
| | 9:10 | The feeding of five thousand hungry people |

(d) *From the world's final limitation—death*

| Luke | 7:11 | The widow's son at Nain* |
|---|---|---|
| | 8:41 | Jairus' daughter |

*Note*   Miracles related only in Luke are marked with an asterisk.

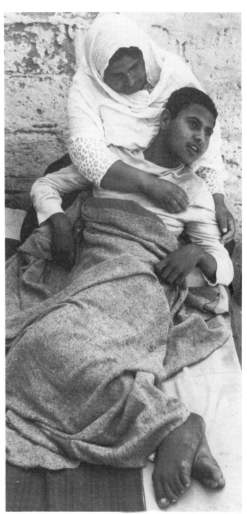

A seventeen-year-old Palestinian boy, paralysed from the age of nine

It is important to realize that the emphasis of these miracle stories is not on their remarkable character. The Gospel writers saw them as visual *signs* that the power of God to save people was at work in Jesus. Jesus, himself, was quick to point out that anyone who was open to the love and power of God could do such remarkable things.

Luke tells his readers again and again that the love and power of God is made present in the world by the compassion, understanding and sympathy that people show for one another. That is the kind of life Jesus led. Luke shows Jesus turning with compassion and understanding to all those who were on the fringes of society, the outcasts, the weak, those possessed by devils, the sick, the sinners—in fact all those who were considered to be burdens on society.

It is interesting to note that there were devout religious groups at the time of Jesus who quite specifically *excluded* these outcasts from their communities. The Qumran monks had a rule excluding madmen, lunatics, simpletons, fools, the blind, the maimed, the lame, the deaf and minors, from entering into the community.

By his words and actions Jesus taught the exact opposite. He loved these outcasts and called them his community. It is this that is unusual, extraordinary and 'miraculous'.

There are some scholars who think John the Baptist may have joined the Qumran community for a while. If this was so, no wonder he couldn't really make Jesus out. When he sent messengers to Jesus asking, *'Are you the one.... or should we expect someone else?'* (Luke 7:19), Jesus replies with words reminiscent of the *Manifesto*:

> *The blind can see,*
> *the lame can walk,*
> *those who suffer from dreaded skin-diseases*
> *are made clean,*
> *the deaf can hear,*
> *the dead are raised to life*
> *and the Good News is preached to the poor.*
>
> Luke 7:22
> cf Isaiah 35:5–6

What a contrast to the spirit of Qumran! It is this, says Luke that makes Jesus unique. What he was saying and doing was quite unusual in his time.

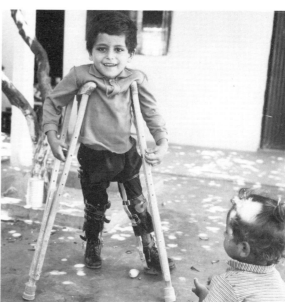

New leg braces mean a brighter future for this refugee boy

## Further Issues

Until recently Christians have usually accepted the miracle stories as descriptions of what actually happened. Today scholars question whether the stories should be taken so literally. Is it any longer possible to know what really happened?

The New Testament uses three Greek words for our word 'miracle'.

1. The most common word is *dynamis* which means a work of *power*. The actions of Jesus show the power of God working in him. God's power is always to save.
2. Often the word *semeion* is used. It describes a *significant* event, one which pointed to the fact that God was at work.
3. Sometimes the word *teras* is used. It means a *wonder*, an astonishing· work, something to marvel at.

None of these words suggest that what Jesus did violated the universal laws of a fixed nature. The definition of 'miracle' given on page 31—'an event or an action which violates the laws of nature'—is one which was only adopted in the 18th Century. It is only in the last 200 years or so that Christians were expected to believe that Jesus was able to suspend the laws of nature.

The Roman Catholic Church in a solemn meeting of their bishops (the First Vatican Council, 1870) went so far as to call 'anathema' (which means condemned as heretical) anyone who says that miracles can't be fully understood, or anyone who doubts that they *prove* the divine origin of Christianity.

It is this very late interpretation of miracles that has led many Christians to think of Jesus as a magician who could 'turn on' his supernatural powers when he wanted to. He was God in human clothes who could do anything he wanted.

This concept of Jesus has led some people to disregard him altogether, and others to believe that the miracles attributed to him are only superstitious legends. He was, to them, just a good man.

The world today is not the world of the 18th or 19th century, still less the world of the New Testament. Today's scholars understand and interpret the world in a new way, a way opened up by science, medicine and psychology. They are not necessarily being irreligious or lacking in faith if they seem reluctant to allow a miracle to be 'a miracle'. What have they got to say about Jesus the wonderworker?

1. Jesus clearly worked wonders. The evidence for the miracles is as sound as the evidence for his teaching.
2. The miracles were certainly never proofs that he was God. People in New Testament times accepted their reality quite simply, and expected any prophet to work similar wonders. And Jesus said that his disciples would work even greater wonders.
3. In a pre-scientific age anything that could not be explained as 'natural' was attributed to the 'supernatural'. Some of these 'supernatural' happenings can now be given a natural explanation. Even St Augustine of Hippo (died AD 430) said: *'Miracles are not contrary to nature, but only contrary to what we know about nature.'* A modern theologian, Gregory Baum, says: *'Miracles occur at the edge of the possible.'* (*Man Becoming*, Herder and Herder, 1971)
4. In his teaching Jesus insisted that God's Kingdom was to be found, not in the heavens, but amongst people. The gospel writers saw that the Kingdom of God had come in the human life of Jesus. It was in his human expressions of love and compassion and acceptance of all people that they saw the presence of God. A Jesus who could call upon supernatural powers at his pleasure does not fit in with this understanding of the gospel.

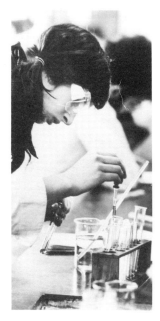

5. The gospel is a proclamation of *faith* in the Jesus who died but still lives on. The resurrection is the key event in the gospel story. The miracle stories are a proclamation of what the risen Jesus meant to the writer. For this reason John La Farge wrote of the miracles: *'For those who believe in God, no explanation is needed; for those who do not believe in God, no explanation is possible.'*

6. *Conclusion.* Modern scholars take the miracle stories very seriously. Professor Barclay calls them *'deep stories rather than tall stories'.* It is impossible to know what exactly happened when Jesus performed miracles. There are many possible interpretations. What is certain is that Jesus did marvellous things out of his love and compassion—so wonderful that many saw in him the presence of God.

John Robinson sums it up:

*For the Christian, Jesus is no semi-divine wonder-worker. He is a man so completely one with the Father that in him and through him no limit can be set to the power of the Spirit of God. And that, he promises, goes also for all who allow that same Spirit to flood and control their lives.'*
*But that I can't believe*, Fontana, 1967

### A closer look at some of the miracle stories in Luke

Luke told these stories with hindsight and in retrospect. It will be impossible to know 'what really happened'. We will look at possible explanations and try to discover what the stories meant to Luke.

### Miracles peculiar to Luke

Luke has five miracles in his Gospel which do not appear anywhere else. They are all stories in which Jesus has compassion on the sufferings of individuals. They are given new life and hope through their brief contact with him. The five miracles are:

| | |
|---|---|
| Luke  7:11 | The widow's son at Nain |
| 13:11 | A crippled woman |
| 14:2 | A sick man |
| 17:12 | Ten men with skin disease (lepers) |
| 22:50 | The High Priest's slave |

It is curious that one of these miracles takes place in the Garden of Gethsemane at the arrest of Jesus. It is curious because this scene is described in some detail in all four Gospels. But only Luke has the miracle (See Luke 22:51). Why?

Mark reports that one of Jesus' disciples drew his sword and cut off the ear of the High Priest's slave. Matthew tells the same story and adds that Jesus rebuked the disciple saying, *'All who take the sword will die by the sword.'* Luke tells the same story but Jesus rebukes the disciple more gently, and tells us that it was the right ear that was cut off, and that Jesus healed the man.

Most scholars feel that Luke is being quite free in his telling of the well-known story. He wants to emphasize that throughout the terrible events of his arrest Jesus remained compassionate and thoughtful of others. Luke is going to make the forgiveness of enemies a theme in his passion account. It begins here with a miracle of forgiving compassion. What actually happened? We have *no* means of knowing. Nor is it necessary to know. The important thing for the Christian is to discover what Luke is wanting him to know about Jesus.

## The Feeding of the Five Thousand
Read the text carefully in Luke 9:10–17.

*Some points to note*
1. This is the only miracle recorded in all four Gospels. Mark and Matthew even record it twice.
2. It is worth comparing the texts to see what variation Luke introduces (Compare Matthew 14:13–21; Mark 6:30–44; John 6:1–14). The following points are interesting:

   (a) Luke mentions 'the *twelve* disciples'. The others do not mention numbers. The miracle story is placed by Luke in the section of the gospel where he clearly has the organization of the early church in mind (See page 43).

   (b) Mark says that Jesus took 'pity' on the crowd. Luke says that Jesus '*welcomed*' them. This is a Lukan word. He makes Jesus more open and accepting of others. Remember that his privacy is being invaded!

   (c) Only Luke says that Jesus spoke to the crowds about the *Kingdom of God*. The theme is dear to Luke.

   (d) On careful reading it is clear that Luke re-arranged some sentences in the story to make it run more smoothly. His work is *more polished* than the others. For example, he mentions the crowd of five thousand in verse 14 where he needs to emphasize the amount of food needed. Matthew and Mark keep that information until the end—for dramatic effect.

   (e) Luke *softens the story* a little. The disciples sound less irritable.

   There are many ways in which this story could be explained. Here are some of them. What do you think?
1. It could be an accurate account of an astonishing prodigy whereby Jesus literally multiplied bread out of a few sandwiches.
2. It could be a highly exaggerated story where perhaps only a few hundred people shared a small quantity of provisions.
3. Jesus' words were so hypnotic that no one noticed that they only nibbled a few crumbs.
4. It could be a story that comments on the marvel of people sharing with one-another. John Robinson gives an example of a group of young people who decided to trust in a miracle of sharing—or go hungry. They found that people were willing to share, and commented, '*That hillside must have been a riot of conversation and laughter two thousand years ago* '

5. An 18th century German theologian even offered this curious explanation. He suggested that Jesus had a band of secret disciples whom he met in caves in the desert. In one cave they kept a large supply of provisions. This incident took place just near that cave, so Jesus had easy access to a large supply of bread. A more recent suggestion is that Jesus was standing near the entrance to the cave where the Qumran community kept their stores. And he helped himself from it.

6. C. H. Dodd thought the story may have a political background. The crowds were trying to attract Jesus to the cause of the Zealots. Jesus refused their offer of kingship by inviting them all to share a symbolic meal. For such a meal only a little bread is needed. He was showing them that the Kingdom of God had come when people shared with one another. The earliest account of the event (Mark's) ends with the disciples *amazed* because they couldn't understand the meaning of what Jesus did (Mark 6:52). Dodd suggests that this phrase gave the whole story an air of mystery and so it came to be described as a spectacular event when it really hadn't been.

7. It could be a completely symbolic story, with no historical basis. The Gospel writers were reflecting on Old Testament expectations and on the eucharistic practices of the early church.

*Conclusion*

Many of these 'explanations' remove all the mystery from this story, and some Christians repudiate them for that reason.

The only question we are really entitled to ask is, what did the story mean to Luke? And we must appreciate that he is retelling the story to people who have experienced Jesus die and rise in glory.

So it is never going to be possible to know the historical facts that lie behind the story. From what we have discovered of Luke it is clear that this miracle story is his way of telling people that the Kingdom of God had come amongst them. The Isaiah *manifesto* was being realized. The hungry were being fed; the poor did not have to pay; there was bread enough for all who came. And it was Jesus who made this possible.

---

As you read all the miracle stories in Luke remember that he was only interested in the value these traditional stories had for conveying *his* idea of Jesus.

For Luke the 'miracle' about Jesus was that he made God real to those who took him seriously and met his challenge.

For many Christians today 'miracles' are those events which make God real to them. Remember Mary-Anne at the beginning of this chapter. Nothing fills her more with wonder than the birth of a baby. In that ordinary event she is made aware of the presence of God. Luke knew exactly what Mary-Anne means. Why else did he write of the 'miraculous' birth story of Jesus?

## A   Quick answers

1.   In which town was Jesus when he ordered an evil spirit to leave a man?
2.   To whom did Jesus say, *'Don't tell anyone, but go straight to the priest and let him examine you.'*?
3.   Who said *'Go away from me, Lord! I am a sinful man!'*? What miracle had he witnessed?
4.   Who was Jairus?
5.   Which miracle story is told immediately after the scene of the transfiguration?
6.   When Jesus healed the man with a paralysed hand why was he being watched very closely?
7.   What really surprised Jesus about a Roman officer?
8.   Where does Luke place the 'Feeding of the Five Thousand'?
9.   What happened at Nain?
10.   Where did Jesus heal a blind beggar?
11.   How many of the ten lepers went back to thank Jesus for their cure?
12.   How many miracle stories are found only in Luke's Gospel?

## B   Longer answers

1.   The miracle stories fall naturally into four groups. Describe the four groups and give an example for each group.
2.   What is similar about the stories describing the healing of a man with a paralysed hand and the healing of a crippled woman?
3.   In how many of the twenty-five miracle stories mentioned in Luke does the need for *faith* appear?
4.   Describe in your own words the story of the man from Gerasa, who was possessed by demons.
5.   *'Go and tell John what you have seen and heard'* (Luke 7:22).
What had they seen and heard? Why did Jesus send this message to John?

## C   Essays

1.   Write about one miracle in each case where Jesus is said to have shown his power over (a) nature, (b) disease, (c) death.
Comment on the reasons why he is said to have performed each of these miracles.
2.   Describe what happened when Jesus healed (a) a young boy or girl, and (b) a man suffering from leprosy or blindness.
What place did *faith* have in both stories?
3.   *'Modern readers of the Gospels find accounts of Jesus' cure of disease easier to believe than those about his control over nature.'* Do you agree with this statement? In your answer describe at least one example of both types of miracle story.
4.   Read Luke's story of Peter's miraculous catch of fish (5:1–11). It takes place when Jesus calls his first disciples. Look at how Matthew and Mark describe this calling of the first disciples (Matthew 4:18–20; and Mark 1:16–18). They don't mention the miracle of the fish. Can you account for this?
5.   An Argus poster reads: *'Miracles happen only to those who believe in them.'* Comment, with some reference to Luke's Gospel.

## D   For individuals and groups to do

1.   Make a collection of art pictures (postcards?) which depict the miracles in Luke's Gospel.
2.   There are twenty-five miracle stories in the list on page 33. Use twenty-five sheets of paper (perhaps A4 size) to make a collage of *one* of the miracles on each sheet. (No repeats!) As far as possible use contemporary material from magazines and newspapers. Display as a mural, five sheets by five sheets.
3.   Find out some miracle stories from other traditions Jewish, Islamic, Buddhist, Hindu, etc.

# B5 The journey

## The Way In

Have you read *Pilgrim's Progress* by John Bunyan? Bunyan, a 17th century tinker, was sent to prison for his Baptist preaching. There he wrote the story of a pilgrim's **journey** from this world to the next. There are many books where a journey runs through the whole story. Try to think of some.

One of them, *I am David*, was written this century, in 1965, by Anne Holm. The story is the long and lonely *journey* of David, the boy from the concentration camp who sets out to find himself.

> *Then a warm wet feeling on his face woke him up.*
> *It was not the farmer after all! It was the dog who wanted to go with him!*
> *It trotted along by his side, sometimes running on ahead but always returning to keep him company, and every time he spoke to it, it would wag its tail.*
> *David breathed deeply, hardly noticing the cold bite in the air. He was David. He was free and strong. He was on the move again, but this time he knew where he was making for. There might be many difficulties ahead before he reached his goal, but difficulties could be overcome. He still had one more promise of help left over from God, and he had the dog who was going with him of its own free will. The long winter had passed, and he was going down to meet the spring.*
> Methuen, 1965

Luke is another one of those writers who finds that a *journey* is a useful way to tell a story. A journey has a starting place and a goal—a place of arrival. In the story *I am David* it is very clear that David's journey is really a search for his identity. But perhaps all the other journey stories are also to do with people searching to discover more about themselves? You might know some more stories like this.

## Main Issues

*'As the time drew near when Jesus would be taken up to heaven, he made up his mind and set out on his way to Jerusalem'* (Luke 9:51). For ten chapters Luke takes us on a *journey* with Jesus, from Galilee to Jerusalem. The section beginning here in Chapter 9 finishes in Chapter 19. It is, in fact, quite an artificial arrangement. Why did Luke write it in this way?

### 1. The importance of Jerusalem

We have already seen on page 26, that Luke wants to give dramatic emphasis to Jerusalem. He concluded his infancy narrative with a journey to Jerusalem. He wanted to be quite sure that his readers were pointed in the right direction from the start. Here he uses over a third of the Gospel for a journey that has Jerusalem as the goal. He reminds us, now and again along the way, that Jesus is going to David's city. The signpost 'To Jerusalem' is repeated ten times. *'As Jesus made his way to Jerusalem he went along the border between Samaria and Galilee.'* (Luke 17:11).

### 2. A useful framework

This travel story is a literary device. Luke is not interested at all in the route Jesus follows. He is just interested in the goal. He is emphasizing that Jesus was on a journey to his death in Jerusalem.

Luke uses this journey to introduce much of the material which Matthew and Mark do not have. He doesn't tell us very much about what Jesus did (although a few miracles are included), he is most interested in the teaching of Jesus. He gathers together many short sayings and parables of Jesus and he uses the journey as a thread to string them on. He describes how Jesus taught the crowds in the villages and towns and how he talked to the apostles and disciples as they travelled together. The section contains some of the finest stories in the Gospels, like the Good Samaritan (10:25–37) and the Prodigal (Lost) Son (15:11–32).

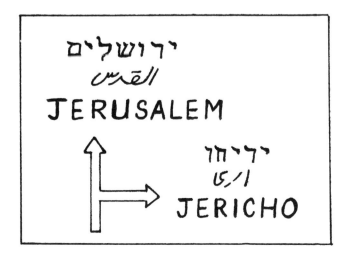

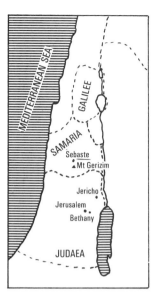

### 3. Vague geography

It is obvious that Luke isn't describing an actual journey that Jesus took—the geography is all wrong. First of all, places don't fit. He starts out from Galilee by the short route through Samaria, but arrives by the longer route through Jericho. He seems to arrive in Bethany, a few miles from Jerusalem, long before he crosses the borders of Samaria and Galilee. Look at Luke 10:38–41 and Luke 17:11. From John's Gospel we can identify the 'village' of Luke 10:38 as Bethany. Luke leaves place names deliberately vague. *'Jesus went through towns and villages teaching the people and making his way towards Jerusalem'* (Luke 13:22).

### 4. Sense of urgency

There is, at moments in the journey, a sense of urgency. It certainly starts that way. Jesus *'made up his mind and set out on his way to Jerusalem'*. Luke conveys the feeling that Jesus is earnestly driving himself forward and urging his disciples to do the same.

In 9:57–62 three would-be disciples are told that they would have to be uprooted from any security and not even the slightest delay can be allowed.

Chapter 10 begins with 72 (some manuscripts say 70) disciples being sent out by Jesus. They are urged to move quickly, no time for change of clothes or even to pass the time of day!

After the return of the 72 disciples in Chapter 10, the sense of urgency subsides, but it is resumed as the journey comes towards Jerusalem, it end, in Chapter 19.

### 5. Journey starts with the Samaritans

Luke starts this important journey section with a quite deliberate description of Jesus shocking his companions. There was a long standing feud between the Jews and the Samaritans. The symbols of their bitter hostility were the rival temples on Mount Zion in Jerusalem and on Mount Gerizim in Samaria (see page 8). Samaritans showed their antipathy towards Jews most strongly when they were on their journey to Jerusalem.

When, in verse 54, James and John asked Jesus if they should call fire down from heaven to destroy the Samaritans, they were acting as Jews had always felt—following the example of Elijah, who had done just that (See 2 Kings 1:9–16).

The rebuke Jesus gave was astounding to the Jews. He was showing towards Samaritans a compassion and acceptance unheard of before.

Luke shows how the gospel does reach Samaria later, in his second volume, the Acts of the Apostles.

# Further Issues

### Christ's journey and the Church's journey

Scripture scholars point out that although Luke's journey theme forms a section of its own (9:51–19:44), it begins inside another and more intricate theme.

Look at the third paragraph of the journey, at 10:1ff. The 72(or 70) disciples are sent out. Does it remind you of the sending out of the 12 disciples at 9:1ff? Look more closely and see the pattern which emerges.

Mission of the Twelve 9:1
            Passion Foretold 9:21
                Transfiguration 9:28ff.
            Passion Foretold 9:44
Mission of the Seventy-two 10:1

The transfiguration, from a 15th Century Italian bible

It is probable that Luke meant the *transfiguration* to be the centre point of his gospel, on which the whole story of Jesus turns (See pages 83 and 115). He has framed that central story with two scenes in which Jesus sends out his disciples. We can tell how artificial that framework is by comparing Luke to Mark (whom he is copying). In order to allow the clear pattern above to emerge, Luke has had to omit the three whole chapters which Mark has placed between the transfiguration and the sending out of the disciples (Mark 6:7 to 9:2) What is Luke up to?

Luke writes his first volume with the second volume in mind. The story of Jesus is the pattern on which the story of the Church is to be based. In volume 2 (Acts of the Apostles) the whole Christian community will go on a Christ-like journey to bring men to the presence of God.

> (Luke) is tying the history of the church (represented by the 12 and the 70) into the history of Jesus... The tie up of Christians with Christ is made particularly strong by being done on both sides of the main transfiguration block.
>
> J. Drury *Luke* Fontana, 1973

Why twelve disciples and then 72(70)? Luke wants to show the gradual expansion of Jesus' mission. The Good News is first told by, and to, the twelve tribes of Israel. But it is eventually meant for all the 72(70) nations of the world (See Genesis 10). When Jesus instructs the 72(70), he is giving a missionary guide to the early church. And Luke will tell us a lot more about that in his second volume (Acts).

D

**A troubled Jesus?**

Read again the following texts:

Luke 12:49–53
Luke 18:31–34
Luke 19:41–44

What do you notice? Luke is giving us here a rare glimpse into the mind and heart of Jesus. There is a dark, agonized and troubled spirit in Jesus. He yearns to bring God's message, to set the world ablaze with the fire of it. But at what a cost to himself!

Remember that Luke had already framed his transfiguration scene with two scenes in which Jesus predicts his death (Luke 9:21 and 44).

Luke frequently underlines the paradox in the story of Jesus:

his power and his weakness;
his acceptance by people and his rejection;
his glory and his suffering;
the understanding of his followers and the misunderstandings.

Followers of Jesus would have to expect the same.

*If anyone wants to come with me, he must forget self, take up his cross every day, and follow me. For whoever wants to save his own life will lose it, but whoever loses his life for my sake will save it.*

Luke 9:23–24

*Do you suppose that I came to bring peace to the world? No, not peace, but division.*

Luke 12:51

**Conclusion**

Religious people very often use the *journey* as a symbol of movement towards a goal (truth). Here are just a few examples.

1. In the book of Genesis there is the *journeying* of Abraham (Genesis 12ff).

2. The most important event in Israel's history is the *Exodus*—the departure from slavery in Egypt and the long journey to freedom. (Book of Exodus) It is still re-lived by the Jews in their Passover celebration.

3. Gautama, founder of Buddhism in the 6th Century BC, spent the whole of his middle years journeying and searching for 'enlightenment'. Having discovered it, he spent 45 years *journeying* through India to teach others.

4. Lao-tze, reputed founder of Taoism, in the 7th Century BC is said to have spent his whole life *journeying* through China before ascending to heaven.

5. One of the five Pillars (religious duties) of a Muslim is called the 'Hajj'. This is a *pilgrimage* to the Holy City of Mecca. Every Muslim is expected to make this journey once in a lifetime. Muhammad, was himself a *traveller*.

6. Luke uses the journey theme to show his readers that they are to be travellers (pilgrims) on the way to God. Note:

the *journey* of the boy Jesus to Jerusalem;
the *journey* section of the Gospel;
the *journey* of Jesus to Calvary;
the *journey* of the disciples to Emmaus;
the *journeying* of the early Christians in Acts.

7. The churches have readily taken up the symbol and Christians have always called themselves *pilgrims*. In the 12th century actual pilgrimages (journeys to holy places) became popular. Kenneth Clark commented:

> *No good pretending they were like cruises or holidays abroad. For one thing they lasted far longer, sometimes two or three years. For another, they involved real hardship and danger. In spite of efforts to organize pilgrimages, elderly abbots and middle-aged widows often died on the way to Jerusalem.*
>
> K. Clark *Civilization* B.B.C., 1969

Percy Dearmer's hymn (after John Bunyan) is still a favourite today in many churches:

*He who would valiant be*
*'gainst all disaster,*
*let him in constancy*
*follow the master*
*there's no discouragement*
*shall make him once relent*
*his first avowed intent*
*to be a pilgrim.*

*Since, Lord, thou dost defend*
*us with thy Spirit,*
*we know we at the end*
*shall life inherit.*
*Then fancies flee away!*
*I'll fear not what men say*
*I'll labour night and day*
*to be a pilgrim.*

*Percy Dearmer (1867–1936)*
after John Bunyan (1628–88)

## A   Quick answers on the text

1. Why wouldn't the people in Samaria receive Jesus?
2. A teacher of the law, wanting to justify himself, asked Jesus a question. What did he ask?
3. Name the two sisters who received Jesus into their home.
4. What did Jesus say to the woman in the crowd who praised his mother?
5. What incident caused Jesus to tell the story of the Rich Fool?
6. Jesus healed a crippled woman on the Sabbath. How long had she been ill?
7. Whom did Jesus call 'a fox'?
8. When the Pharisees and teachers of the Law grumbled: 'This man welcomes outcasts and even eats with them,' Jesus told a parable. Which one?
9. What happened to the rich man and to Lazarus in the parable?
10. What was surprising about the one leper who was grateful for being cured?
11. Who was Zacchaeus?
12. Why did Jesus drive merchants out of the Temple?

## B   Longer answers

1. The word Jerusalem is mentioned twelve times in this section (as a kind of signpost). Find the references and write down the chapter and verse for each one.
2. Write out the words of Jesus to the three would-be followers (9:57–62).
3. Tell in your own words the parable of the Great Feast.
4. When does Luke use the journey theme in his writings? (*Note*: at least 5 times)
5. Why is it obvious that Luke isn't describing an actual journey in his 'journey section'? What is it about then?

## C   Essays

1. Describe and explain the parable of the Dishonest Steward (Shrewd Manager). Give two other examples of the teaching of Jesus on wealth.
2. Luke tells us that Jesus sent out 70(72) of his followers. What instructions did he give them and what was said on their return.
3. Describe Jesus' conversation with (a) a man of the ruling class (a ruler or Jewish leader), and (b) Zacchaeus. Why would Luke be interested in telling of these conversations?
4. Would Christians today make more impact on people if they lived in less comfort, as Jesus suggests in 9:57–62?
5. In Chapter 15 Luke deals with 'lost and found', a father and his ill-behaved sons. So does Deuteronomy 21:15–22:4. Study both texts and write some comments on what you find.

## D   For individuals and groups to do

1. Make a classroom frieze on the journey theme.
2. Prepare a ten-minute assembly on 'Pilgrimage'. (Work alone or as a group).
3. Find out what you can about the journeying of one of the following: (a) Gautama (b) Muhammad (c) Lao-tze. Prepare to tell the rest of the group/class about it.

# B6 Jerusalem

## The Way In

The Mayor of Jerusalem, Teddy Kollek, invited children of the world to do a painting of the Holy City. This picture of Jerusalem was done by a twelve-year-old Israeli girl.

In a foreword to a book of the best paintings, Danny Kaye wrote:

*Jerusalem the legendary, Jerusalem the golden; the goal, the centre, the shrine of three of the world's major religions. Ever since it was stormed and taken by King David in 1000 BC the city has inspired painters, poets, prophets, and pilgrims, not to forget the philosophers and politicians with their visions of peace and dreams of empire.*
        *Children of the World Paint Jerusalem* (Bantam and Keter, 1978)

Twelve-year-old Avigail Matalon sees Jerusalem as a 'valentine to peace'. Here is how a modern Israeli poet sees the city.

### A SONG FOR JERUSALEM (Yerushalayim)

*The evening breeze upon the hillside, the sweet perfume of pine,*
*The bells which chime out in the distance intoxicate like wine;*
*And in a dream of towers and treetops, walled in by sleeping stone,*
*Jerusalem, the waiting city, lies silent and alone.*
    *Yerushalayim bathed in light, bathed in bronze and bathed in gold,*
    *What am I but the harp on which your songs are told?*

*But when I come to sing your praises with words fit for a king,*
*I am a child who cannot speak yet, a poet who cannot sing.*
*For your name needs a choir of angels, your glory to unfold;*
*Jerusalem, if I forget you. . . . city of purest gold.*
    *Yerushalayim bathed in light, bathed in bronze and bathed in gold,*
    *What am I but the harp on which your songs are told?*
                                        Naomi Shemer, 1967
                            Tr. H. J. Richards and N. Brummer

For the Jew there is always a yearning for Jerusalem. Jews throughout the world long to go there. This is nothing new. Look at Psalm 137. In 597 BC Jerusalem fell to the Babylonians and from their captivity the Jews sighed for their homeland. (Zion is another name for the Holy City.)

*By the rivers of Babylon we sat down;*
*there we wept when we remembered Zion. . . .*

*How can we sing a song to the Lord*
*in a foreign land?*
*May I never be able to play the harp again*
*if I forget you, Jerusalem!*

Throughout history, Jerusalem has been a bone of contention between rival powers. It has been captured and recaptured. You probably know about the Crusades. It is a city that has been written about with affection, with tears, with sighs and with admiration.

*'Let Jerusalem come into your mind, remember, Lord.'*

*Weep today the bitterest tears,*
*Pour thy heart, grief, tell thy fears,*
*'Tis the day of wrath and shame:*
     *Jerusalem!   Jerusalem!*

*Kings and Princes, all are ta'en;*
*They who fought for thee are slain;*
*What is left thee but thy name?*
     *Jerusalem!   Jerusalem!*

*See! the foes thy walls have gained,*
*Zion's Temple is profaned,*
*Fort and tower are wrapped in flame!*
     *Jerusalem!   Jerusalem!*

from *The Liturgy of the Templars**

*Dear Carey,*
     *We arrived here a fortnight ago. The weather is not yet too hot. It is an astonishing place. Words fail me. I can't begin to describe it. There is a mad balance (preserved by Brit. Govt.) between ancient and utter loveliness and mod. bestial commercial enterprises—in fact they cancel out. There is also a mad confusion of religions, all worshipping and scrapping at same shrines.*

Eric Gill (written in 1934)*

*He came closer to the city, and when he saw it, he wept over it saying, 'If you only knew today what is needed for peace! But now you cannot see it. The time will come when your enemies will surround you with barricades, blockade you, and close in on you from every side. They will completely destroy you and the people within your walls'.*

Luke 19:41–44

*Touching Jerusalem as a whole it certainly looks rather striking from the Mount of Olives across the Valley of Jehoshaphat, but it is like all other Eastern cities, a dreary network of covered streets with stalls at each side; and the surrounding country is all the same colour as the houses. . . . . We have seen the Church of the Holy Sepulchre, where the Sepulchre, Calvary, the place where the rock was rent by the earth-quake, the centre of the earth, and about thirty-five other things all conveniently brought together under one roof. I am sick of traditions.*
     The Letters of William Henry Leighton (1826–1883) to his brother*

* These items are from *The Image of Jerusalem* (Uni of Rochester, N.Y., 1968)

Knights of the first Crusade
1096–1099

*The Lord built his city on the sacred hill;*
*more than any other place in Israel*
*he loves the city of Jerusalem.*
*Listen, city of God,*
*to the wonderful things he says about you. . .*

*Of Zion it will be said*
*that all nations belong there*
*and that the Almighty will make her strong.*
*The Lord will write a list of the peoples*
*and include them all as citizens of Jerusalem.*
*They dance and sing,*
*'In Zion is the source of all our blessings'.*

Psalm 87

*I had always dreaded the day when I should have to leave Jerusalem, but*
*the reality was sharper than I have ever dreamed. . . .*
*I cannot pretend to describe or analyse my love for Jerusalem. It is not*
*wholly sentimental, aesthetic or religious—still less theological or*
*archaeological; though I hope it contains something of all five. A little*
*perhaps also that I had worked there and enjoyed and suffered there*
*from the beginning; that I knew the people so well and liked them so*
*much; that after misunderstandings had always followed under-*
*standing. . . . . For me Jerusalem stood and stands alone among the cities*
*of the world. There are many positions of greater authority and renown*
*within and without the British Empire, but in a sense that I cannot*
*explain there is no promotion after Jerusalem.*

Sir Ronald Storrs (British Governor) Orientations, 1943

## Main Issues

### The magnetism of Jerusalem

Jerusalem casts an extraordinary spell over everyone who visits it.
Tourists and pilgrims will tell you that it is really quite unlike any other
city. It has a magnetism which is impossible to describe.

A donkey emerging from
a suq

They dance and sing in Jerusalem

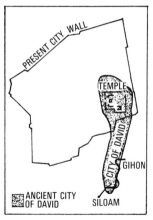

ANCIENT CITY OF DAVID

Jerusalem is a sacred city for Jews, Christians and Muslims. It is the city where Solomon built the Temple, where Jesus preached and died, and where Muhammad dreamed of the Dome of the Rock.

The visitor to Jerusalem today sees an old walled city, known as East Jerusalem. The name West Jerusalem is given to the mainly Jewish town outside the walls.

You may have seen pictures on TV of Arab life within the walls of the Old City today. It is easy to suppose that nothing much has changed since the time of Jesus. In fact the city has seen many changes. The two maps show how the city boundaries changed, even between David's time and Jesus' time.

The present city walls are only about 450 years old but they rest on foundations another 450 years old, the work of the Crusaders. You can see from the map that the Jerusalem of Jesus' time was about the same size (about 1 km. across at its widest point), but lay 500 metres south. The ancient city of David was much smaller.

The importance of the city for the Jews began with its capture by David.

*The time came when King David and his men set out to attack Jerusalem. The Jebusites, who lived there, thought that David would not be able to conquer the city, and so they said to him, 'You will never get in here; even the blind and the crippled could keep you out,' (But David did capture their fortress of Zion, and it became known as 'David's City'.)*

2 Samuel 5:6–7

CITY IN THE TIME OF JESUS

Arabs in Jerusalem market

The time chart will give you an idea of how the city changed hands over the centuries.

| | | Some Key Dates |
|---|---|---|
| BC | 1000 | David's city |
| | 950 | Solomon's Temple built |
| | 586 | Destruction by Babylon |
| | 520 | Second Temple built |
| | 160 | Maccabee revolution |
| | 20 | Herod's Temple built |
| AD | 30 | Jesus' ministry and death |
| | 70 | Destruction by Rome |
| | 135 | Roman city |
| | 335 | Holy Sepulchre church built |
| | 687 | Dome of the Rock built |
| | 1099 | Crusader Kings of Jerusalem |
| | 1516 | Turkish walls built |
| | 1920 | British Mandate begins |
| | 1948 | State of Israel established |
| | | Divided Jerusalem |
| | 1967 | United Jerusalem |

Jerusalem, David's city, in New Testament times stretched from the Temple (now the Dome of the Rock) down to the trees in the foreground

## The importance of Jerusalem

Jerusalem is the focal point of the history of God's people. It is also the focal point of Luke's Gospel.

Jerusalem was not simply the capital city: the City of David; it was, above all, the Holy Mountain where God had chosen to enter into communion with man. It was the City of the Lord because of the Temple. This is how it was seen by the pilgrims who went to Jerusalem to 'seek the face of God'.

*I was glad when they said to me,*
*'Let us go to the Lord's house.'*
*And now we are here,*
*standing inside the gates of Jerusalem! . . .*

*Pray for the peace of Jerusalem:*
*'May those who love you prosper.*
*May there be peace inside your walls*
*and safety in your palaces.'*

Psalm 122

The Western Wall

For Luke, Jerusalem is of enormous importance.

1. He starts his Gospel there, unlike the other gospel writers. He begins his story with Zechariah, the priest, serving in the Temple.

> *One day Zechariah was doing his work as a priest in the Temple, taking his turn in the daily service. According to the custom followed by the priests, he was chosen by lot to burn incense on the altar.*
>
> Luke 1:8–9

2. Then Luke completes the infancy narrative with the story of Jesus lost and found on the third day, in the Temple at Jerusalem. Is it meant to remind us of the resurrection from the dead on the third day—in Jerusalem?

> *Every year the parents of Jesus went to Jerusalem for the Passover Festival. When Jesus was twelve years old, they went to the festival as usual. When the festival was over, they started back home, but the boy Jesus stayed in Jerusalem.*
>
> Luke 2:41–3

3. We have already seen that Luke places ten chapters of his Gospel in the framework of a journey towards Jerusalem. To reach that city is the goal. At least ten times he includes the signpost 'to Jerusalem'.

> *As the time drew near when Jesus would be taken up to heaven, he made up his mind and set out on his way to Jerusalem.*
>
> Luke 9:51

4. It is interesting that for Luke, the risen Jesus stays in Jerusalem. The story finishes where it started. Mark and Matthew have resurrection stories in Galilee.

5. It is no surprise that Luke begins Volume 2, The Acts of the Apostles, in Jerusalem. He starts there and then expands across the whole world.

The young Jesus preaching in the Temple, from a 15th Century Italian bible

# Further Issues

## A spiritual Jerusalem

Do you know this old hymn, 'Jerusalem the Golden'?

> *Jerusalem the golden,*
> *With milk and honey blest,*
> *Beneath thy contemplation*
> *Sink heart and voice oppressed.*
> *I know not, oh, I know not*
> *What joys await us there,*
> *What radiancy of glory,*
> *What bliss beyond compare....*
>
> *O sweet and blessed country,*
> *The home of God's elect!*
> *O sweet and blessed country*
> *That eager hearts expect!*
> *Jesus, in mercy bring us*
> *To that dear land of rest;*
> *Who art, with God the Father*
> *And Spirit, ever blest.*

Bernard of Cluny, tr. J. M. Neale (1819–66)

Bernard lived in the 12th century, but from the very beginning of the Christian church Jerusalem became the focus of a Christian mysticism. It became *the* symbol of the heavenly future. Already in the 4th century *St Augustine* wrote:

> *Jerusalem, my happy home,*
> *Name ever dear to me!*
> *When shall my labours have an end,*
> *In joy, and peace, and thee?*

This idea of Jerusalem as a heavenly city, as distinct from the physical city in Palestine, was already hinted in the prophetic writings of the Old Testament. Ezekiel had a great vision of a future Jerusalem with a rebuilt Temple, set in the midst of all nations.

A model reconstruction of Herod's Temple

*I will put my Temple in their land,*
*where it will stay for ever.*
*I will live there with them;*
*I will be their God,*
*and they will be my people.*

Ezekiel 37:27

This spiritual significance of the city of God captivated people's minds. Generations of poets and writers have portrayed the Holy City as the essence of all that is good and beautiful.

*May the desire of the heavenly Jerusalem grow and be strong in our hearts, that we be not tossed on the streams of Babylon of this world of confusion.*

Prayer from an ancient manuscript

*Then I saw a new heaven and a new earth. The first heaven and the first earth disappeared, and the sea vanished. And I saw the Holy City, the new Jerusalem, coming down out of heaven from God, prepared and ready, like a bride dressed to meet her husband.*

John in Revelation 21:1

*So part we sadly in this troubled world*
*To meet with joy in Sweet Jerusalem.*

Shakespeare in *Henry VI*, iii.

### Jerusalem Today

The historical city of Jerusalem is beautiful. It has a fine position on the Judaean heights; it has a gentle climate; it has its walled compactness and eastern charm. But for all this, it is always a city of tension. You will often see it reported in the news because of clashes between the Israeli and Arab population. If Jerusalem is important to the Jews it is no less important to the Arabs. Here is a very sensitive Arabian legend about the city.

*When Jerusalem was still only a ploughed field, the corner on which the Temple now stands was owned by two brothers, one married with several children, and one a bachelor.*

*Together they grew corn on their field, and at harvest time stacked their sheaves next to each other. That night, the unmarried brother said to himself, 'My brother has a wife and children to support. It's not fair that I should have as much corn as him. I will take a few sheaves from my stack and add them to his. He won't notice, so he will have them without knowing.'*

*While he was doing this, his married brother woke up and said to his wife, 'My brother has no wife and children to help him and brighten his life. It's not fair that we should have as much corn as him. Let's go and add a few sheaves to his stack. He won't notice, so he will have them without knowing.'*

*The next day, when the brothers came to the field to work, they were both surprised to find the stacks equal, but said nothing. But that night, and for the rest of the week, they both got up and went out on the same errand.*

*Finally, unable to understand why the stacks remained equal, they both stayed up to watch. And so the two brothers met, each carrying sheaves to the other's stack.*

*In memory of their generosity, a house was built in this field to the name of God.*

How is it that both Arabs and Jews lay claim to this land? The original close relationship between these races is described in a picturesque way in the book of Genesis. Both the Arab and the Jewish nations are descended from Abraham, through his two sons. The Arabs are the descendants of Ishmael and the Jews of Isaac (See Genesis 21:9–13).

For many centuries the Arab population lived at peace with the small Jewish communities that had settled there. It is only since the State of Israel was created in 1948, against the will of the Palestinian Arabs, that there has been tension, and sometimes bitter conflict.

## A Divided City

The old city is divided into four 'quarters' by its two main streets. These four sections are in the hands of four different groups.

A Greek Orthodox priest

1. *The Christian quarter*
Many Arabs are Christian. They and their European Christian brothers and sisters belong to different sects (Greek Orthodox, Coptic, Syrian, Maronite, Roman Catholic, Protestant etc). But for all of them Jerusalem is sacred because it is the city where Jesus preached, died and rose from the dead. The Church of the Holy Sepulchre which commemorates the death and resurrection of Jesus is visited by pilgrims from all over the world.

2. *The Muslim quarter*
Jerusalem is sacred to the Muslims because it was important to Muhammad. The Temple area today houses two mosques. (a) The Dome of the Rock is on the hilltop chosen by David for the place of worship. It is sacred to Muslims because tradition identified the bare rock as Mount Moriah where Abraham was willing to sacrifice Isaac, and Muslims venerate Abraham. (b) The El-Aksa Mosque is where the Muslims gather for prayer. It commemorates the 'distant' journey made by Muhammad on his winged horse before ascending to heaven.

3. *The Jewish quarter*
Jews today cannot enter the Temple area because it is in Muslim hands. They gather instead at the *outside*, along the Western Wall. There the area has recently been cleared to provide a vast open-air synagogue. The district to the West has for centuries been inhabited by Jews. Since 1967 it has been restored in a tasteful and sensitive way.

Jews

An Armenian priest

4. *The Armenian quarter*

The area once occupied by Herod's Palace is now the quarter of the Armenian Christians. They are a persecuted people (two million Armenians have been massacred this century), and they have set down deep roots in this land of their exile.

Given so much diversity in one very small city it is surprising that there is so little trouble. Of course there *is* tension but Teddy Kollek, who became mayor in 1967, has written:

> *The outstanding fact today in Jerusalem is the relative tolerance and the veritable ease with which people live in neighbourly relations within the city, in spite of great differences of opinion and great differences of aspiration.*

Essay 'Present Problems and Future Perspectives'

Arab market in Jerusalem

## A  Quick answers on the text

1. Which King of Israel first conquered the city of Jerusalem?
2. How often did the parents of Jesus go to Jerusalem for the Passover festival?
3. In Luke's story of the boy Jesus getting lost in Jerusalem, where was he found?
4. Some Pharisees told Jesus that Herod wanted to kill him. What did Jesus say about Jerusalem in his reply to them?
5. When Jesus reached Jerusalem for the last time he went to the Temple. Why was he angry at what he saw there?

## B  Longer answers

1. Describe in your own words Jesus' triumphal entry into Jerusalem.
2. Why did Jesus weep over Jerusalem?
3. Write a paragraph pointing out Luke's interest in Jerusalem.

## C  Essays

1. Show, by means of clear illustrations, how Luke's Gospel gives a prominent place to Jerusalem.
2. Is it significant that Luke's resurrection appearances of Jesus all take place in or near Jerusalem?
3. Describe in detail the story of the visit of Jesus to Jerusalem when he was twelve. Comment on any *two* points of special interest to you.
4. Retell the stories of (a) Jesus' visit to Jerusalem when he was twelve years old *and* (b) Jesus' entry into Jerusalem near the end of his life. Why do you think Jesus acted as he did in each of these incidents?

## D  For individuals and groups to do

1. Collect as much information about Jerusalem as you can and display it in an attractive way.
2. Find out about the reasons behind the creation of the 'State of Israel' in 1948.
3. Invite someone who has visited Jerusalem to come and talk to your class/group.
4. Here is a poem by a modern Israeli poet, Shin Shalom. He is writing about the Arab/Israeli conflict. What is he saying? (Read Genesis 21 as well.)

*Ishmael, my brother,*
*How long shall we fight each other?*

*My brother from times bygone,*
*My brother—Hagar's son,*
*My brother, the wandering one.*

*One angel was sent to us both,*
*One angel watched over our growth—*
*There in the wilderness, death threatening*
*   through thirst,*
*I a sacrifice on the altar, Sarah's first.*

*Ishmael, my brother, hear my plea:*
*It was the angel who tied thee to me....*
*Time is running out, put hatred to sleep.*
*Shoulder to shoulder, let's water our sheep.*
*Forms of Prayer for Jewish Worship* Shin Shalom
(1904–1977)

'How long shall we fight each other?'

# B7  *The passion and death of Jesus*

Inexpensive badge

## The Way In

Pilgrims to Jerusalem today arrive by jumbo jet at Tel Aviv airport. Many thousands of Christians fly in at Easter-time to celebrate the death and resurrection of Jesus in the holy places. When they return home they nearly all wear their Jerusalem crosses which can be inexpensive badges or silver and jewelled 'crusader' crosses. In earlier centuries pilgrims trudged their way across Europe on foot to reach Jerusalem. Some came late in their lives, hoping to die there. And many did. The little crosses they wore have been dug up in their thousands, like the little Byzantine cross shown.

Silver and jewelled Crusader cross

Russian pilgrims at a baptism ceremony, by the Jordan, around 1890

Why would all these pilgrims wear a cross? Because the cross was seen as the *sign* which says most clearly what Christianity is about. Yet down the ages, the same sign said different things to different people. We can see this in the way artists have represented the cross, through the ages.

Here is one of the earliest known attempts (about AD 400) to portray Jesus on the cross. It is an ivory carving on a very small box in the British Museum. The figure though stiff, is not dead. Did the artist think that Jesus didn't really die, or that his death was unlike any human death, because he was God? We'll never know the answer of course. It's interesting to look at other artists' representations of Jesus' death.

Early Byzantine cross

a

b

c

d

e

a Russian silver-gilt crucifix, 18th Century

b Grünewald cross, 16th Century

c Lothar cross, 10th Century

d Irish Celtic cross

e Marc Chagall's 'White Crucifixion', 1938, (Oil on canvas; 61″×55″; a gift from Mrs A Alschuler) © The Art Institute of Chicago, All Rights Reserved

f Crucifix from the Ramsey Psalter

f

E

## Main Issues

How does Luke tell the story of Jesus' passion (suffering) and death?

### 1. Jesus enters Jerusalem

The great drama begins with his triumphant approach to Jerusalem. Read Luke 19:28ff. The account is rich in Old Testament references. It is taken basically from Mark though Luke has adapted it. What does it all mean?

Prophets were accustomed to making dramatic gestures when their words seemed to have fallen on deaf ears. (See 1 Kings 11:29ff; Jeremiah 27:1–11; Ezekiel 4:1–3.) Luke says Jesus performed just such a dramatic action by riding into Jerusalem on the donkey. Many followers of Jesus would have expected him to be proclaimed Messiah in Jerusalem, and to bring about the reign of God by first defeating the Romans. The ride into Jerusalem was to show that this was a mistaken expectation.

As in many other incidents it is difficult to know exactly what really happened.

Children enact a procession for Palm Sunday

(a) If this was a *historical event*, Jesus presumably set up the occasion with careful planning. Yet even in that context, for a wanted man to enter the city so publicly was a clear act of defiance. Was Jesus then deliberately contriving to fulfil the words of Zechariah (9:9), by proclaiming himself as Messiah?

> *Rejoice, rejoice, people of Zion!*
> *Shout for joy, you people of Jerusalem!*
> *Look, your king is coming to you!*
> *He comes triumphant and victorious,*
> *but humble and riding on a donkey,*
> *on a colt, the foal of a donkey.*
>
> (Matthew and John actually quote this text)

(b) It is always possible that it was the *evangelists themselves who linked the Zechariah text with Jesus*—in retrospect. In this view Jesus rode the donkey into the city rather unnoticed precisely because other pilgrims were doing the same!

Luke echoes the note of joy in the Zechariah text by adding verse 37 (where the disciples praise God with loud voices). It is Luke too who introduces the word 'king' (Zechariah 9:9) in verse 38. *God bless the king who comes in the name of the Lord! Peace in heaven and glory to God.* This of course is also an echo of the angels' song at the birth of Jesus.

So the story is, above all, about peace. Kings rode to battle on horses; when they came in peace they rode on donkeys. Jesus, by his action, was coming into Jerusalem as a lover of peace, not as a conquering military hero. If the disciples wanted a national leader to free them from the Romans, they would have to find someone other than Jesus.

It is only Luke who concludes this episode with Jesus weeping over the city. Jerusalem means 'foundation of *peace*' and Jesus was politically shrewd enough to see that the fall of the city was becoming inevitable. The city he loved so much would be anything but peaceful. In AD 70 it did fall to the Romans.

The long journey to Jerusalem is over, and the destination has been reached. This is a great moment for Luke, so he trims away Mark's notes about Jesus coming and going between Jerusalem and Bethany: the city is reached and entered once and for all.

Jesus is in Jerusalem to undergo his passion and to die. Luke has been reminding us of this since Chapter 9. See especially 18:31:

> Listen! We are going to Jerusalem where everything the prophets wrote about the Son of Man will come true. He will be handed over to the Gentiles, who will mock him, insult him, and spit on him. They will whip him and kill him, but three days later he will rise to life.

## 2. Jesus is questioned

Once in Jerusalem Jesus goes to the Temple and immediately the confrontation with the authorities begins. Chapter 20 of Luke is sometimes known as the 'Day of Questions'. While Jesus is in the Temple four questions are posed.

### (a) *A question of authority* (Verses 1–8)
The chief priests, teachers and elders set a trap for Jesus, asking him by whose authority he acts. Jesus turns the argument by questioning his questioners. He confronts them with the authoritative figure of John, asking their reaction to him. They are caught out because they cannot commit themselves and so, in turn, cannot press Jesus further.

### (b) *A question about paying taxes* (Verses 20–26)
The chief priests and law teachers try again to get Jesus to compromise himself with Roman authority. Jesus again compromises his opponents: he doesn't even carry a Roman coin as they do! He cannot be accused of collaboration or causing rebellion. He side-steps trouble, makes it clear he is not a political leader and shows that people can loyally serve both God and their nation.

### (c) *A question about rising from death* (Verses 27–39)
Now the conservative Sadducees (see page 8) ask a question—a ludicrous one. The Pharisees believed in a general resurrection of the dead, the Sadducees didn't. So the Sadducees quoted a teaching of Moses in Deuteronomy and invent a hypothetical situation that makes the idea of resurrection look ridiculous. Jesus shows how the Sadducees are confusing the conditions of earthly and heavenly existence. Even the teachers of the Law are in admiration of Jesus' skill in answering the question.

(d) *A question about the Messiah* (Verses 41–4)

Jesus turns the tables. He asks a question, quoting Psalm 110, which Jews regarded as referring to the Messiah. If David called the Messiah 'my Lord' he was thinking of someone more exalted than himself. As no father would call his own son 'Lord' how can the Messiah be a son or descendant of David? Jesus forces the authorities to analyse their understanding of the Messiah. Their view is not the same as Jesus' view.

They are now set on a collision course.

### 3. Jesus' last supper

Read Luke 22:1–38. When a person dies, their family and friends usually look back and remember with special emotion the last occasion when they sat down and spoke together, or had a meal together.

The early church treasured the memory of the last meal that Jesus had with his disciples, and commemorated it by re-enacting it, in a simple way. This became the characteristic worship of the Christian church. Today the ceremony is known by different Christians as the Eucharist, or the Communion Service or the Mass.

The 'last supper' Jesus had with his friends was not just an ordinary, everyday meal. He had arrived in Jerusalem at the time of the Passover Feast. 'Passover' was *the* great Jewish festival. Celebrated on the 15th Nisan (full moon, around our March/April), it commemorated the setting free of the Jewish people from slavery in Egypt. During the special meal the events recorded in Exodus, Chapter 12 were recalled:

> *When your children ask you, 'What does this ritual mean?' you will answer, 'It is the sacrifice of Passover to honour the Lord, because he passed over the houses of the Israelites in Egypt. He killed the Egyptians, but spared us.'*
>
> Exodus 12:26–7

This Passover meal began a festival *week*, known as the Feast of Unleavened Bread (See Exodus 12:15–20). Jerusalem was always crowded for the festivals as pilgrims came from everywhere to celebrate in the holy city. (They still come today—from all over the world!)

Participants in a Passover meal

Trouble was always expected as national feelings ran very high. Crowd trouble is nothing new.

This is the background to the last days of Jesus' life. The authorities resolved to arrest Jesus. They wanted to do it in secret for fear of causing riots. Judas Iscariot, a disillusioned disciple, gave them the opportunity they needed (verses 3–6).

Luke gives no reason for Judas' betrayal. (John attributed it to greed.) Some speculate that Judas was a militant Zealot (See page 8) who became impatient with Jesus' non-violent line, Luke says simply that *Satan entered Judas*. It was a battle between God and Satan, between good and evil.

### The meal itself

The last supper Jesus had with his friends was sometime during the festival. This makes it special and his followers were quick to see the symbolism in it.

But it is not clear from the Gospels on *which day* Jesus had this meal.

Verses 7–13 describe the preparation for the meal and it is a description of the normal preparation for the Passover meal. But the lambs were always slaughtered a day *earlier* (14th Nisan) than the meal, whereas Luke makes everything happen on the *one* day. He obviously wasn't as interested in the details of the festival as he was in the symbolism: Jesus' important last meal coincided with a festival commemorating the setting *free* of people. This is exactly how Luke saw Jesus—the one who set people free.

It is interesting that John looked at it from another viewpoint. He places the crucifixion of Jesus a whole day earlier than the Synoptic writers. He probably wanted to portray Jesus dying exactly at the time when the Passover lambs were being killed in the Temple. Why would he want to do this?

Part of the confusion about time may arise from the fact that different Jews may have used different calendars for celebrating their feasts. Certainly they used a different time system from the one we have inherited from the Romans. They reckoned days as beginning and ending at sunset. So although Christians commemorate the Last Supper on the Thursday evening of Holy Week (as it is called), Jews would call that Thursday evening, early Friday.

### Some notes about the meal

Remember that Luke is using the earlier writings of Mark, but as usual he freely adapts him.

(a) He expands the story of the supper by adding the teachings of Jesus. He uses the table scene as an opportunity for teaching rather than for eating. Luke has always liked banquet scenes where people communicate in words.

(b) It is Luke who names the two disciples who prepare the Feast—Peter and John.

(c) It is only Luke who begins the meal with the welcoming words: *I have wanted so much to eat this Passover meal with you before I suffer!*

(d) Verses 19 and 20 read:

Sleeping disciples from a
mosaic in St Mark's, Venice

'This is my body, which is given for you. Do this in memory of me. In
the same way, he gave them the cup after the supper, saying, 'This cup
is God's new covenant, sealed with my blood, which is poured out for
you.'

In some early manuscripts of Luke's Gospel the words immediately
after 'This is my body' are omitted. It is possible, therefore, that the
words were not written by Luke but by the early church. They knew
Paul's account of the Last Supper and wanted to use these words in
their memorial services. Look at Paul's words in 1 Corinthians
11:24–5. Compare them with Luke.

(e)  It is typical of Luke that he changes the order of Mark's account. He
keeps the words of Jesus about the betrayal until the *end*. This
allows the supper scene to be more serene than Matthew's and
Mark's (they bring in the prediction of betrayal at the start of the
meal). And Luke leaves out the terrible words of Mark: '*It would
have been better for that man if he had never been born.*'

(f)  Verse 24. Luke introduces the argument about greatness here. He
does so to establish the theme of Christian community, (fore-
shadowed in 5:1–11). The church here is really given its charter
and its charge—to be at the service of others. And Luke projects the
community he imagines around the table into the future (verse 30).
For him the Last Supper is an image of the great feast that God will
give (Isaiah 25:6–8).

(g)  It isn't surprising that Luke says something about Peter here. He
will show in the early chapters of Acts that Peter's primacy in the
Church is one of service to others.

(h)  The instructions about swords, found only in Luke, are surely
meant ironically. In the Middle Ages the church allegorized the
scene, saying Jesus was giving to the successors of Peter the two
swords of spiritual and civil authority. This is *not* what verses 24–7
mean!

## 4. Jesus in agony

Read Luke 22:39–46. Again Luke's account of the agony of Jesus differs from
Mark.

(a)  Luke does not call the garden
'Gethsemane'—simply the Mount of
Olives.

(b)  The disciples replace Peter, James
and John.

(c)  They are asked to pray '*so that you
will not fall into temptation*' (reminiscent of the Lord's Prayer 11:4).
Luke repeats this at the end of the
scene, to frame the episode.

(d)  It is typical of Luke that he softens
Jesus' words to the sleeping disciples. He does not repeat the rebuke
and has Jesus offer a kindly interpretation for their sleeping—
emotional exhaustion.

The Garden of Gethsemane

(e) Verse 43. The appearance of an angel is found only in Luke. It is Luke's way of emphasizing that God *was* with him.

(f) Verse 44. Also peculiar to Luke. The sweating that was so heavy that Jesus seemed to 'bleed' with sweat, emphasizes the extreme anguish and desolation Jesus was suffering. If Luke was a doctor he knew about such physical manifestations of fear. Some manuscripts leave out this verse—perhaps afraid to portray Jesus at his most human!

This scene leads immediately to Jesus' arrest. In all that follows Luke is going to show that Jesus was a 'good and innocent man'. He edits Mark's dark and rather ambiguous narrative and simplifies it. He is going to bring back his familiar themes of repentance, forgiveness, tenderness and the compassionate humanity of Jesus.

## 5. Jesus is arrested and is crucified

Naturally, each of the four evangelists tells the story of Jesus' arrest, trial and death. But they all tell the story differently. Scholars have always puzzled over the inconsistencies—with no definite conclusions. Here we simply outline the series of events as Luke records them, noting his particular style and approach. (The numbering corresponds with that on the map.)

(1) *Jesus is arrested* (Luke 22:47–53)
A crowd of people, led by Judas Iscariot approach Jesus. Jesus sadly reproaches his friend, Judas, with the words *'Judas, is it with a kiss that you betray the Son of Man?'* As we already saw on page 36 Luke portrays Jesus as healing the slave wounded by one of the disciples. Jesus is compassionate and merciful, even in his time of suffering.

(2) *Before the High Priest* (Verses 54–63)
He is taken to the High Priest (Caiaphas, but not named by Luke). Peter, following behind, warms himself at the fire in the courtyard. But, frightened at what was happening he denies he knows Jesus. Luke adds two telling touches of his own to the account—*'The Lord turned round and looked straight at Peter,'* and the adverb 'bitterly', describing how Peter wept.
Jesus is then mocked and beaten by the High Priest's guards.

Giotto's 'Kiss of Judas'
(detail)

### (3) *The trial* (Verses 66–71)

Luke says that the trial began only at daybreak. The elders, chief priests and teachers met together in *council* (known as the *Sanhedrin*) and Jesus was brought before them. It is not clear if Jesus was taken to the Sanhedrin building.

The trial begins with the crucial question '*Are you the Messiah?*' But Jesus makes it clear that they weren't really interested; they were only interested in finding an excuse for getting rid of him. Jesus' reply is neither an admission nor a denial. People must make up their own minds.

### (4) *Jesus before Pilate* (Luke 23:1–6)

The Council feel they have heard enough—they could charge him with blasphemy. But it is only Rome that can convict, and Rome needs a political motive and not a religious one. So Jesus is sent off to Pilate. An accusation is made that he claims to be the 'Messiah, a *king*'. Jesus again avoids a direct answer.

Luke is anxious to defend Christianity as being no danger to Rome. '*I find no reason to condemn this man*', says Pilate (verse 4). He is to repeat this defence of Jesus three more times (verse 14, 15 and 22).

*Note*   It is not clear historically where Pilate held his court. A strong tradition believes he was residing in Fortress Antonia. But another tradition favours Herod's Palace.

### (5) *Sent to Herod* (Verses 7–12)

Only Luke has the trial before Herod. He suggests that Pilate stalls for time by sending Jesus to Herod (because Jesus was a Galilean and Herod ruled over that region). Herod treats the whole affair lightly. He and his soldiers mock Jesus and show their contempt by putting a fine robe on him. Jesus is sent back to Pilate and Luke says that Pilate and Herod became friends. Here Luke takes the blame for the mockery of Jesus away from the Romans.

### (6) *Sentenced by Pilate* (Verses 13–25)

Back goes Jesus to Pilate. In Luke's description of this trial it is clear that he is concerned to clear the reputation of Pilate (who stands for the Roman Empire) as best he can. Pilate makes three declarations of Jesus' innocence and suggests the minor punishment of whipping, so that Jesus can then be let off. The inflamed crowd want Barabbas set free—an ironic situation because his crime was clearly political. Pilate, too weak to stand by his convictions, gives in and sentence is passed.

### (7) *Jesus is crucified* (Verses 26–31)

Jesus is *sent* out to be crucified. Luke, like Mark and Matthew, tells how Simon is ordered to help carry the cross. Only Luke adds that Simon had to walk *behind* Jesus. He is acting out the discipleship of 9:23 and 14:27.

Then Luke combines three of his interests in a scene peculiar to himself. Women, the city and the unfolding of history come together when Jesus meets the group of mourners. He says that the future must be terrible, if things can happen like this in fairly peaceful times.

The Way of the Cross today

(8) *Crucified with two criminals* (Verses 32–48)

Jesus is crucified with two criminals. Luke alters Mark in order to make the executions explicitly simultaneous. It is only Luke who has the conversation between Jesus and one of the criminals (known now as the 'good thief'). It is so typical of Luke—here is another repentant sinner, like the prodigal son or Zacchaeus.

Again it is only Luke who has Jesus' prayer of forgiveness for his executioners. It is not unlike the prayer of Stephen at his death in Acts 7:60.

Jesus dies a calm and dignified death. The anguished cry, *'My God, my God why have you forsaken me?'* of Mark is replaced by *'Father! in your hands I place my spirit!'*

Mark has described a darkness that covered the earth at this time. Luke uses the striking symbol of an eclipse of the sun. In the ancient world, events both great and tragic were often described as accompanied by portents of nature.

Finally Luke sums up for his readers how he sees Jesus. The army officer speaks for him saying: *'certainly he was a* good man.' This is not what Mark had recorded earlier. For him the officer said: *'He really was the Son of God.'*

And it is only Luke who concludes the sad scene with the crowd being quietly converted.

## Further Issues

What does the death of Jesus mean?

The death of Jesus was understood, from earliest times, as the most important event in his life. Christians speak of it as being their 'salvation'. They are 'saved' by the cross. How can what someone did 2000 years ago affect people's lives? How can the death of Jesus put people in the right relationship with God?

Christian thinkers through the ages have used different images to explain this belief.

Crusader crosses, Church of the Holy Sepulchre

### 1. Satisfaction theory
God is like a judge in a law court. He is just and impartial, only interested in the law itself. Justice demands that the wrongs (introduced into the world by people's sin) must be redressed. The demands of this just God are met by Jesus on mankind's behalf. He makes the satisfaction owed by mankind.

### 2. Propitiation theory
In this view God is no longer impassive, he is very *angry*. His plan for the world has been spoilt by sin. Someone needs to calm God down. Jesus takes that role on and by his innocent death he soothes God's anger.

### 3. Sacrifice theory
The idea of sacrifice is much older than Christianity. In many ancient religions gods and goddesses were offered sacrifices (even human ones) in the hope that these would re-establish right relations with the god. The Jews of the Old Testament frequently made sacrifices to God. Numerous lambs were sacrificed each day, and at Passover the special Passover lamb was slaughtered. It is not surprising that the Christian Church was quick to identify Jesus as a sacrificial 'Passover lamb'.

### 4. Redemption theory
Jesus is very frequently called the 'Redeemer'. The image developed in the Church of Jesus 'buying' people out of their slavery, which is sin. (We redeem our possessions out of the pawnbrokers when we can pay for them.)

### 5. Atonement theory
This theory is about a transaction between two parties, God and man. They have got to be brought together. It was Anselm (1033–1109) who said '*God became man*' to bring about this reconciliation. God had been injured by sin and man had caused the injury. Only a 'God-man' could put God and man 'at one'.

It is interesting how the old hymn writers made use of all these theories. Here is an example from the 11th century.

*Bring, all ye* dear-bought *nations, bring,*
*your richest praises to your king,*

*alleluia, alleluia,*

*that* spotless Lamb, *who more than due,*
paid *for his sheep, and those sheep you,*
*Alleluia.*

*That guiltless Son, who* bought *your peace,*
*and made his Father's* anger *cease,*

*alleluia, alleluia,...*

*O thou, whose power o'ercame the grave,*
*by grace and love us sinners* save
*Alleluia.*

*Wipo (11th C.)* tr. Walter Kirkham Blount

Few Christians today find these images very helpful. This is understandable because they were written in earlier ages when the world view was quite different. They were also based on secular, legalistic language. But they shouldn't be dismissed as useless descriptions of the reality. They show how people have struggled to speak of the God who is beyond all human thinking.

In all these images it is *God* who demands Jesus' death. There is little of this in the New Testament. The authors there turn more easily to the image of 'revelation'. It is to this notion, of Jesus' death *revealing* God, that many theologians look today to understand Jesus' death and its effect on the world.

Jesus reveals a new understanding of God. He embodied godliness in a human life. Where people had thought of God as distant and judgemental, Jesus portrayed God as being close, compassionate, forgiving, merciful and understanding.

This portrait of God was seen clearly in the life of Jesus himself. And nowhere was this more evident than in his accepting even death on a cross, without hitting back. For it wasn't God who demanded that death, but sinful men. God forgives even the death of his son.

A Christian believes that this understanding of God, for those who accept it, changes everything.

It frees people from their burdens.

It brings them close to a God who is their loving father.

It inspires them to be, in their turn, compassionate, forgiving and merciful.

From our analysis of Luke's portrait of Jesus, we can see how sympathetic he is to such an explanation. Jesus' death is *salvation* because it wonderfully draws people close to God and each other.

'If you are cut down in a movement that is designed to save the soul of a nation, then no other death could be more redemptive.'
Spoken by Martin Luther King, one of the great Christian champions of human rights, who was himself assassinated 4 April 1968, aged 39

## A   Quick answers on the text

1. Where did Jesus and the disciples eat the Passover meal?
2. Who denied knowing Jesus?
3. Who carried Jesus' cross for him?
4. In which place was Jesus arrested?
5. Where, according to Luke's account, did the ascension take place?
6. What title did Pilate order to be put above the cross of Jesus?
7. How did Judas plan to identify Jesus to the people who wanted to arrest him?
8. Who placed the body of Jesus in a tomb?
9. What did Jesus cry out just before he died?
10. Who was Barabbas?
11. Who put *'a fine robe'* on Jesus?
12. Who said *'certainly he was a good man!'*?

## B   Longer answers

1. Describe, in a paragraph, the attitude of Pilate at the trial of Jesus.
2. Describe how Jesus entered Jerusalem for the last time.
3. Describe the two criminals who were crucified with Jesus.
4. Outline the sequence of events from Jesus' arrest to his death.

## C   Essays

1. Give an account of the Last Supper and the teaching that Jesus gave after it in the upper room (according to Luke).
2. Write a full account of the crucifixion as told by Luke. Comment on the words spoken by Jesus.
3. Describe the examination and trial of Jesus before (a) the Jewish Council, (b) Pilate and (c) Herod. What are the reasons given for these three trials?
4. On the cross Jesus was rejected and despised; he forgave his tormenters, comforted his companions and impressed a centurion. Describe this in as much detail as you can.
5. Comment on the charges brought against Jesus before Pilate. What efforts did Pilate make to set him free?
6. Describe in detail the parts played by (a) Judas Iscariot, (b) Pilate and (c) Herod during the last days of Jesus.

## D   For individuals and groups to do

1. In ·groups, collect representations of the cross (ones you can cut out) and display them, with your comments.
2. Work out a reading of Luke's Passion for several voices, with background music and slide accompaniment.
3. Make a collage of the cross using contemporary illustrations of suffering, anguish, death.
4. Try to find examples of music written about the Passion and Death of Jesus in different styles: classical, pop, folk and in church hymnals.

# B8 The resurrection

## The Way In

What do you think the following stories have in common?
1. A father's words on the death of his five-year-old son

*I think we owe it to Paul not to dwell entirely on the grief and sorrow. For neither grief, sorrow nor sadness were Paul's life style. Rather he knew not grief nor sorrow, nor sadness, nor suffering, nor sickness, but what he did know from the time he was born until he died in my arms Sunday night, was love. And love he received. And love he gave—in abundance. He knew joy, fun, kindness and concern for everyone. Everyone Paul met was Paul's friend...Paul lived for a party, for a game, for a good time. He was an idealist. He was very sensitive. I believe the only hurt he knew was to see someone sad. And then he would say anything to make them happy.*
*Therefore, I think a worse tragedy than Paul's death would be to measure his life span by the calendar. It's the normal thing to think it's all right to die at eighty but a tragedy to die at five. When we think this way it makes Paul's life look a waste. Paul's life was not a waste. But instead it reached a beauty, and a fullness, and a fruition in five short years that many, if not most, never reach. Paul knew the qualities that this life is all about. Especially what it should be about—love and concern. Therefore, it is our hope and prayer that while you share our sorrow, you will also help in some way to perpetuate, not just Paul's memory, but Paul's style. And in that way, Paul Joseph will live forever.*
T. Newman and P. Stone *Travelling to Freedom* (Living Parish Publication, 1971)

2. An incident in a prison camp in Russia

*During the Russian Revolution, a young woman was put into prison. Days of solitary confinement, nights of interrogation, followed. During one of these nights she felt her strength was failing her, her fortitude and her readiness to stand the test were weakening, and of a sudden she felt hatred and anger welling up in her heart. She wanted to look up at her interrogator, challenge him with all the violence she could muster to break the spell of these endless, hopeless nights of torture, even if she should die for it. She looked up indeed, but she saw nothing, because on the other side of the table, she saw a man as completely exhausted as she was, ashen, worn out, with the same expression of despair and distress on his face, and she suddenly realized that they were not, properly speaking, enemies. Yes, they were sitting on two opposite sides of the table, they were in an irreconcilable tension and opposition, and yet they were both captives of the same historical tragedy, caught up in the same whirlwind of history that had thrown one in one direction and the other in another... And at that moment she realized, because she saw in the other man a victim like herself, that he also was a human being... He was not an enemy, he was a fellow being, caught up together with her, inseparable from her, in the tragedy. She smiled at the man.*
Metropolitan Anthony *Meditations on a Theme* (Mowbray, 1972)

At five months old this little girl weighed only five pounds. She nearly died. Here, at five years old, she is full of life. A resurrection?

### 3. An incident related at the Nuremberg war-crime trials

*In the Nuremberg war-crime trials a witness appeared who had lived for a time in a Jewish graveyard, in Wilna, Poland. It was the only place he—and many others—could live, when in hiding, after they had escaped the gas chamber. During this time he wrote poetry, and one of the poems was a description of a birth. In a grave nearby a young woman gave birth to a boy. The eighty-year-old gravedigger, wrapped in a linen shroud, assisted. When the newborn child uttered his first cry, the old man prayed: 'Great God, has thou finally sent the Messiah to us? For who else than the Messiah himself can be born in a grave?'*

P.Tillich *The Shaking of the Foundations* (S.C.M., 1948)

### 4. An incident in Belfast, N. Ireland

*A young I.R.A. sympathiser, Michael, was convicted of murder. His distraught mother was in my parish. One evening I answered the door to a lady who looked drawn and tired. She asked me if I could possibly take her to see Michael's mother, as she wanted to share her sorrow. I agreed to take her. Imagine how I felt when I left them together—one, the Catholic mother of the young murderer, the other, the Protestant mother of the young victim. They were both holding hands and weeping with and for each other.*

told to the author by a Catholic priest

### 5. An incident in Moscow in 1941

*In 1941 my mother took me back to Moscow. There I saw our enemy for the first time. Nearly 20,000 German prisoners were to be marched in a single column through the streets of Moscow. The pavement swarmed with onlookers... The crowd were mostly women. Everyone of them must have had a father or a husband, a brother or a son killed by the Germans. They gazed with hatred in the direction from which the column was to appear. At last we saw it. The women clenched their fists. The soldiers and the police had their work cut out to hold them back. All at once something happened to them. They saw German soldiers, thin unshaven, wearing dirty bloodstained bandages, hobbling on crutches or leaning on the shoulders of their comrades. They walked with their heads down. The street became dead silent—the only sound was the shuffling of boots and the thumping of crutches. Then suddenly I saw an elderly woman in broken-down boots push herself forward and touch a policeman's shoulder saying, 'Let me through.' There must have been something about her that made him step aside. She went up to the column, took from inside her coat something wrapped in a coloured handkerchief and unfolded it. It was a crust of black, hard bread. She pushed it awkwardly into the pocket of a soldier, so exhausted that he was tottering on his feet. And now suddenly from every side, women were running towards the soldiers, pushing into their hands, bread, cigarettes, whatever they had. The soldiers were no longer enemies. They were people.*

Yevtushenko *A Precocious Autobiography* (Dutton, 1972)

Many Christians see in these stories a kind of resurrection. Resurrection means 'a bringing back to life'. Perhaps *you* can tell some stories where love and human understanding emerge from darkness, hatred or deep misunderstanding.

When Jesus died a criminal's death his followers were devastated. They were plunged into misery, despair and disillusion. All their hopes for the future seemed shattered. But something happened which changed everything. The first resurrection. *The* resurrection. This is how Luke tells of it.

*Very early on Sunday morning the women went to the tomb, carrying the spices they had prepared. They found the stone rolled away from the entrance to the tomb, so they went in; but they did not find the body of the Lord Jesus. They stood there puzzled about this, when suddenly two men in bright shining clothes stood by them. Full of fear, the women bowed down to the ground, as the men said to them, 'Why are you looking among the dead for one who is alive? He is not here; he has been raised. Remember what he said to you while he was in Galilee: The Son of Man must be handed over to sinful men, be crucified, and three days later rise to life.'*

Luke 24:1–7

## Main Issues

Something happened on the Saturday night and Sunday morning following the death of Jesus. It isn't possible for us to know exactly what that was. Each Gospel has a different version, even of the common material. Matthew and Mark have the appearances of Jesus in Galilee, but not Luke. It all takes place for him, not surprisingly, in Jerusalem.

Read Chapter 24 of Luke. His account of the Resurrection falls into four parts:

The women visit the tomb
The two disciples on the Emmaus road
Jesus appears to the disciples
Jesus is taken up to heaven.

Let us look at these four stories more closely.

### The women visit the tomb (24:1–12)

Although Luke uses Mark's earlier account, the tone of it is completely different. Mark is dramatic. The women are awestruck to find the tomb empty. A young man in white instructs them to go and tell the disciples that Jesus has gone before them to Galilee. They run away terrified, speechless with fear.

Luke is more gentle. The meeting with the messenger(s) in the empty tomb is less sudden. They are told, not to go to Galilee, but to remember what Jesus said when he was in Galilee, that *'The Son of Man must be handed over to sinful men, be crucified, and three days later rise to life.'* The women slowly begin to understand and (unlike Mark's women) actually go to the apostles to tell them. Note especially in this Lukan account:
(a) It is orderly and calm.
(b) It all takes place in Jerusalem; Galilee is only remembered.
(c) The women named are Mary of Magdala, Joanna, Mary the mother of James and companions. (The list is different in the other Gospels.)

(d) In Matthew the message is given by one angel, in John by two angels, in Mark by one man, in Luke by two men. Are these meant to remind us of the transfiguration scene in Luke 9:31? Do they again stand for Moses and Elijah as the representatives of the law and the prophets, now superseded by the risen Jesus?

(e) Verse 12 is a disputed verse. Peter runs to the tomb and sees only the linen wrappings. It may well have been included later to harmonize Luke's account with that of John 20:3–10.

**The two disciples on the Emmaus road** (24:13–35)

Luke gives a detailed account of an event briefly summarized in Mark 16:12–13. This story, about two disciples travelling from Jerusalem to Emmaus on that Easter Sunday evening, is one of the most powerful in the gospel. It is as John Drury has put it '*Luke's last great set piece, bringing together most of the themes he has handled throughout the work.*' (*Luke* Fontana, 1973) The power of this story is in its sense of drama: the ordinary scene works up to a wonderful and exciting climax. It does not set out any explicit teaching, yet it has a power of suggestion which has been appreciated by Christians throughout the ages. The story remains memorable as a story.

Some features should be noted because they are so typical of Luke.

(a) The careful placing of the story in relation to Jerusalem. It begins there and ends there.

(b) The action takes place first on a *journey* then at a *meal.*

(c) There is emphasis on the interior experience of Jesus' disciples.

(d) Jesus, a prophet whose life progressed through suffering to glory, is now the fulfilment of Old Testament prophecy.

(e) The wording of verse 30 (where the disciples recognize Jesus in the breaking of bread) is like the wording of the earliest church services.

Christians through the ages have seen in this story a most powerful expression of their belief that Jesus is really present whenever the *scriptures are read* and whenever the *Eucharist is celebrated.*

Bedouins in their tent

**Jesus appears to the disciples** (24:36–39)

Luke describes an appearance of Jesus to the disciples shortly after his appearance at Emmaus. As they were all discussing what had happened there, he suddenly stood among them, saying, *'Peace be with you'*. The account is similar to the story in John 20:19–21. Like John's, Luke's account is in two halves. The first tells of an appearance and the second of Jesus' last testament to his followers.

In the appearance story there is great emphasis on the flesh-and-blood reality of the risen Lord. *'Look at my hands and my feet and see that it is I myself. Feel me'* (verse 39). It is typical of Luke to balance a sense of the tremendous with a sense of the ordinary. Jesus even eats a piece of cooked fish with the disciples.

This first half of the story, therefore, fixes Jesus and belief in him into people's ordinary, everyday existence.

The second half of the story places Jesus and belief in him into the course of history.

In verses 44–9 Jesus reminds them that he had fulfilled the scriptures. As in the Emmaus story, he opens their minds to understand the events of these past few days. Then he points them to the future—commissioning them to preach to all nations the change of heart which will allow them to accept God's forgiveness. The teaching must begin in Jerusalem. The disciples must remain there waiting for the 'power from above' (the Spirit) promised by the Father.

**Jesus is taken up to heaven** (24:50–53)

The final verses of the Gospel seem to be an account of the ascension of Jesus into heaven. The disciples go with Jesus to Bethany where he blesses them. So he *'departed from them and was taken up into heaven.'*

The words *'and was taken up into heaven'* do not appear in some early texts. If they are genuine, then Luke, like John, sees the resurrection and ascension as one event, occurring on the same day.

A more detailed account of the ascension is given by Luke in Chapter 1 of Acts. There it takes place 40 days after his death. Luke does not seem to be concerned with this discrepancy.

So the Gospel ends with two of Luke's favourite themes, the disciples are filled with great *joy*, and they return to the *Temple*, where the story had all begun.

## Further Issues

*'If Christ has not been raised from death, then we have nothing to preach and you have nothing to believe.'*

(1 Corinthians 15:14)

One of Jesus' early disciples, Paul, wrote this to the Christian community in Corinth. The sentence expresses how fundamental the resurrection is. No one who denies the resurrection can call himself or herself a Christian. But the question still remains: what does resurrection actually consist of? What actually happened after Jesus died?

F

### Evidence in the Gospels

It is quite impossible to get a clear picture from the Gospels of what actually happened *'on the third day'* after the death of Jesus. If the stories are meant to be literal descriptions of what actually took place, then something has gone wrong.

The four accounts of the resurrection are different in many details. It would only be possible to make one coherent account of the resurrection stories by twisting the texts about and by omitting some awkward details. This would be totally dishonest.

Scholars today accept the differences and note that the gospel writers were not embarrassed by them. For example, Luke could, quite happily, have the ascension on day 3 in his Gospel and on day 40 in his Acts. If he could be as free as this about a 'historical' fact, could he be equally free in telling the resurrection stories?

For generations, Christians probably never asked such questions. They presumed the stories to be historical . They took it for granted that Jesus died on Friday and on Sunday his *physical* body came back to life and emerged from the tomb, leaving it empty.

Many Christians today accept this explanation of the gospel stories, and ask no further questions. However, many others wonder whether it is possible to understand the stories in a different way.

### The empty tomb

All four Gospels speak of Jesus' resurrection in terms of an empty tomb. This means that the story is based on a very early tradition. Yet the fact is that our earliest reference to the resurrection makes no mention of a tomb miraculously emptied, only of a Jesus who 'appears' to his disciples.

American Pentecostal pilgrims celebrate the resurrection of Jesus at the 'Garden Tomb'

Paul wrote this to the Christians of Corinth in the year AD 56. (The first Gospel was not written until ten years later):

*I passed on to you what I received, which is of the greatest importance: that Christ died for our sins, as written in the Scriptures; that he was buried and that he was raised to life three days later, as written in the Scriptures; that he appeared to Peter and then to all twelve apostles. Then he appeared to more than five hundred of his followers at once, most of whom are still alive, although some have died. Then he appeared to James, and afterwards to all the apostles. Last of all he appeared also to me. . . .*

1 Corinthians 15:3–8

Paul speaks of resurrection, both here and elsewhere in his epistles, *without* referring to Jesus' tomb at all. That being so, is it possible that the story of a tomb found empty is no more than a highly dramatic way of saying that although Jesus died, he is not among the dead? If people want to find Jesus now, it is no good going to the cemetery. He mysteriously lives on, and is to be found in the midst of his disciples.

In that case, the corpse of Jesus would have nothing to do with belief in his resurrection. The resurrection would not be about Jesus' flesh and bones, but about his 'body', which in biblical language means his closeness to his disciples. The real Christ is not a revived corpse.

### The appearances

All four Gospels speak of the resurrection in terms of a Jesus who appears to his friends after he has died. Paul speaks the same language. But it is interesting to note that he uses exactly the same word for his own 'seeing' of Jesus as he used for the first Easter appearances.

*'He appeared to Peter and then to all twelve apostles. Then he appeared to more than five hundred. . . Then he appeared to James. . . Last of all he appeared also to me.,*

1 Corinthians 15:5–8

We think of the Easter appearances as so physical that any bystander could have seen them too. Yet Paul uses the same word of his own vision of the risen Christ, when his companions could see nothing (see Acts 9:7). Is it possible that in both cases the same reality is being spoken of? An *insight* into Jesus rather than a physical *sight* of him?

In that case, the vivid language used in the Easter stories (a Jesus who can be touched and felt, who talks and eats) would again be no more than a highly dramatic and effective way of stressing that Jesus *was* alive, and not simply *imagined* to be so. There would have been no 'appearance' of Jesus such as people could have filmed. But who could doubt, seeing the way his friends acted, that Jesus was in reality still alive, and had not been silenced by death?

### Death and Resurrection

When the Easter stories are taken literally, the resurrection of Jesus becomes something totally distinct from his death. One event is the opposite of the other. He died on day 1 and rose again on day 3. The resurrection is something added to his death. *As well* as dying, Jesus *also* rose again.

A modern cross depicting the triumph of the resurrection

Although the gospel stories seem to make this distinction, the thinking *behind* the stories does not. In this thinking, Jesus' death and resurrection are one and the same thing. The resurrection is nothing other than the death of Jesus seen through the eyes of God. In the eyes of the world Jesus was dead. In the eyes of God he was now more alive than ever. *'What was from our side death was from the Father's side resurrection.'* (G. Moran *Theology of Revelation* Search Press, 1967.)

The last gospel writer in particular (John), emphasizes the unity of these two themes. He always speaks of the cross as the 'lifting up' of Jesus in glory. The dying Jesus *already* bequeaths his spirit to his disciples (John 19:30). The risen Jesus *still* shows his friends his wounds (John 20:20).

The liturgy of the Eastern Orthodox Church has always kept this unity. The service for the day on which Jesus died is celebrated by carrying a figure of the dead Christ in procession (the Epitaphion). Yet from that figure living flowers are distributed to everyone in the congregation and the choir sings:

> *I magnify thy sufferings*
> *I praise thy burial and thy resurrection*
> *Shouting, Lord, 'Glory to thee, Hallelujah'.*

Even Western Christians, often unknowingly, have acknowledged that Jesus' death and resurrection are not to be separated. The cross on which Jesus died is not an object of shame, but of glory. So they keep it covered throughout Lent, to unveil it again on the day Jesus died. And they call that day not 'Bad Friday' but 'Good Friday'.

### What really happened?

We have been asking what the word *resurrection* actually means. What does it really consist of? What really happened on that first Easter Day?

Non-believers say, nothing happened at all. It was all imagination. Believers say, something really *did* happen to convince Jesus' disciples that his death was not the end of him. But this 'something' is a matter of faith. It can't be proved.

Some will want to express this 'something' in terms of a visibly empty tomb, and appearances that could have been photographed or filmed. On Easter Sunday, anyone could have visited the tomb and seen it was now quite literally empty. And anyone could have met the risen Jesus in the streets of Jerusalem, and would have had to conclude that he was indeed risen from the dead. That is what the Easter stories mean.

Others will want to treat the stories, with all respect, less literally. They are vivid and dramatic ways of expressing what had happened to Jesus in his death. The Jesus who died was not dead and gone. He had come back to his friends, and was even more active among them than he could ever be before he died. Indeed the 'new life through death' that he preached has been proven true, not just once 2000 years ago, but again and again in the history of mankind. People 'saw' him on the first Easter as they still 'see' him again and again in their own experience. Look back again at the stories on pages 71–2. Can you see why some Christians see a link between these stories and the stories of Jesus' resurrection?

## A   Quick answers from Luke's resurrection account

1.  What was the power that Jesus promised his disciples before the ascension?
2.  Who was Cleopas?
3.  Who said: *'Why are you looking among the dead for the one who is alive?'*?
4.  Name three women who went to the tomb?
5.  How far was Emmaus from Jerusalem?
6.  What books of the Old Testament did Jesus use when explaining things to the disciples on the Emmaus road?
7.  When did the two disciples in the Emmaus story recognize Jesus?
8.  What were the first words of Jesus when he appeared to *all* the disciples?
9.  What did the disciples give Jesus to eat?
10.  Jesus told his followers that in his name they had a message to preach to all nations. What was that message?
11.  Where does Luke say the ascension took place?
12.  To where did the disciples return?

## B   Longer answers

1.  Point out at least *three* differences between Luke and Mark in their accounts of the resurrection.
2.  *'Then their eyes were opened and they recognized him, but he disappeared from their sight.'* (Luke 24:31)
    State and comment on how they recognized Jesus. What did they say to each other?
3.  Why do you think the two disciples on the road to Emmaus failed to recognize Jesus at first?
4.  *'They went back to Jerusalem, filled with great joy, and spent all their time in the Temple giving thanks to God.'*
    Where had they been? What had taken place? Why did they go back to Jerusalem?

## C   Essays

1.  Describe the appearance of Jesus to his disciples in the upper room and the event that followed, at Bethany (as recorded by Luke).
    What problems may be caused for a modern reader by Luke's account of these events?
2.  Write a detailed account of the events *on the road* to Emmaus.
3.  Describe carefully (a) the meeting of the women with two men at the tomb, and (b) the resurrection appearance of Jesus to the eleven disciples in Jerusalem. Comment on *one* aspect of *each story* which you find of special interest.
4.  What evidence does Luke give for the resurrection of Jesus?
5.  *'You cannot be a Christian unless you take the Gospel stories of the resurrection absolutely literally.'* Comment.

## D   For individuals and groups to do

1.  (Homework) Everyone in the group asks a Christian friend or acquaintance what they understand by the resurrection of Jesus. What *actually* happened? Report back to the group next week.
2.  Make a collection of art pictures (postcards) illustrating the resurrection.
3.  Can you find any stories from other religions or from folklore which have a resurrection theme?
4.  Compile a list of glimpses of resurrection:
    (a) in everyday life
    (b) in poetry and literature
    (c) in nature
    (d) in music and art

# B9   Characteristics of Luke's Gospel

A Peruvian father and son symbolize Luke's spirit of joy

## The Way In

What is it that makes Luke's Gospel different from the other three? What are its characteristics? They have been touched upon already throughout this book. Now we can put them together. And we can do it with the help of the 17th century, Dutch artist, Rembrandt.

Rembrandt seems to have had a fellow feeling for Luke. He seems to have understood him better than other artists who have illustrated this Gospel. Rembrandt moved religious painting right away from the Italian grand style into the realities of everyday life in his own city, Amsterdam. He knew his Bible thoroughly and made friends with the local Jews, and even attended the synagogues to learn all he possibly could. But he interpreted the Bible stories in the light of what he saw around him. He felt, with Luke, that Jesus was for all ordinary people, especially for the humble and poor. It is this that makes Rembrandt's paintings so warm and Luke's Gospel so readable.

In the above etching 'Christ preaching the forgiveness of sins' Rembrandt has a very Lukan crowd. He has imagined a scene where Jesus teaches about forgiveness. Sir Kenneth Clark, in *Civilisation* said of the painting: *'Sometimes Rembrandt's interpretation of human life in Christian terms leads him to depict subjects that hardly exist in the Bible, but that he felt convinced must have existed,'* (B.B.C., 1969). The artist has got to the very heart of Luke's Gospel in this picture.

Jesus, in Luke's Gospel, is at home with the ordinary people. He seems to prefer the poor and the outcast, though he addresses everyone. Women and children too, gather round him to listen to his teaching of love and forgiveness.

Jesus, in Luke's Gospel, is a very down-to-earth man. He is so human that he needs, again and again, to withdraw from the hustle and bustle of life to regain spiritual strength through prayer.

Jesus, in Luke's Gospel, is a man completely open to the Spirit of God. And anyone, says Luke, who is full of the Spirit is full of joy. Joy is a keynote of the whole Gospel and is emphasized in its final sentence.

## The Main Issues

### Good news for everyone

The Gospel of Luke could perhaps be subtitled 'Good News for Everyone'. It is a recurring theme in the Gospel that the most unlikely people are called into the Kingdom of God.

As we saw already on pages 21–29, Luke sets the scene in his infancy narratives. There he was anxious to show that Jesus is for all people. The angel brings:

'. . . *good news for you, which will bring great joy to* all *the people.'*

(Luke 2:9)

And Simeon blessed God:

'With my own eyes I have seen your salvation, which you have prepared in the presence of all peoples;
A light to reveal your will to the Gentiles and bring glory to your people Israel.'

(Luke 2:30–32)

Luke is giving us a clue to the understanding of his whole Gospel. He is going to tell his readers again and again that the Good News is for *all* people.

### 1. *Ancestry of Jesus*

When he describes the ancestry of Jesus he doesn't go back (as Matthew does) only to Abraham (forefather of the Jews); he goes back to *Adam,* son of God and forefather of all mankind. Jesus, he says, is not only for the Jews, he is for all people.

### 2. *The message of John the Baptist*

John's message was also a universal one. Luke takes up the words of Isaiah to describe John:

'Get the road ready for the Lord;
make a straight path for him to travel!
Every valley must be filled up,
every hill and mountain levelled off.
The winding roads must be made straight,
and the rough paths made smooth.
All mankind will see God's salvation!'

(Luke 3:4–6; cf Isaiah 40: 3–5)

John's audience included tax-collectors and soldiers. These outsiders were as welcome as anyone.

### 3. *Hostile Samaria*

Luke has Jesus travelling in Samaria as well as in Judaea and Galilee. For Matthew this was not so. *'Do not go to any Gentile territory or any Samaritan towns,'* says Jesus in Matthew 10:5. Luke insists that Jesus came to break down barriers like this (Luke 9:51–6). He alone tells us of the story of the leper who was a Samaritan (Luke 17:12–19). He alone tells the story of the Good Samaritan (Luke 10:30–37).

### 4. *Luke and women*

To read the other Gospels you would wonder if Jesus had any contact with women. Only Luke seems aware of this half of humanity! Luke (perhaps because he was a doctor) wrote sympathetically of Elizabeth, Anna, Martha and Mary, the Widow of Nain, the bent woman and of course of the mother of Jesus, who does not figure in Mark and is completely silent in Matthew.

### 5. *The poor and sinners*

Luke tells us, above all, that it is the least and the lost to whom Jesus preaches the Good News. His is the Gospel of the poor and weak. His infancy story sets the scene. His narrative is about the poor and humble, the shepherds who were outcasts.

The poor and sinners were lumped together. This was because it was supposed that the poor must have been sinners and that a sinner must end up poor. Both were outcasts with no chance of being included in the fold. It is then quite revolutionary to suggest, as Jesus did, that these very outcasts were closer to the Kingdom of God. Religious people were outraged at the suggestion. Luke was thrilled at it.

Luke is the only evangelist to tell us about:

A woman, a sinner, who washed the feet of Jesus (7:36–50).

Zacchaeus, the sinner, who received Jesus into his home (19:1–10).

The good thief, the sinner, who is forgiven on the cross (23:43).

The last words of Jesus '*Father, forgive them...*' (23:34).

And only Luke tells us parables about:

The prodigal son forgiven (15:11–32).

The lost coin found (15:8–10).

The publican preferred to the Pharisee (18:9–14).

Lazarus the poor man in glory (16:19–31).

Hiyam and her brother, two out of some four hundred thousand Palestinian child refugees

### Luke and prayer

> '*At daybreak Jesus left the town and went off to a lonely place. The people started looking for him.....*'
>
> (Luke 4:42)

Luke gives us a picture of Jesus as a man who had the need to get away from crowds and pressures in order to be still and to reflect. He seems more aware of this aspect of Jesus' life than the other evangelists are. Luke was deeply aware of the humanity of Jesus, and all human beings need the space for quiet and reflection.

1. *Important events*

It is, above all, at the most important moments of his life, that Luke shows us Jesus at prayer.

(a) At the start of his public life when he was being baptized (3:21).

(b) The night before he called the Twelve (6:12).

(c) At the time that he called for Peter's great act of faith (9:18).

(d) Before he set his face towards Jerusalem, when he was 'transfigured' (9:28).

(e) Just before his capture and trial when Luke emphasizes the earnest and agonized prayer of Jesus (22:39–45).

2. *The transfiguration* (Luke 9: 28–36)

There is a subtle difference between the way Luke tells the story of the transfiguration and the way the others tell it. Luke alone says that Jesus went up the mountain *to pray* (9:28). The prayer transfigures Jesus and gives him a foretaste of the resurrection.

To pray like this is to enter into God's world and to reflect its light. For Luke it all happens *to* Jesus. The scene is about his prayer.

Matthew and Mark make it sound as though Jesus set up the whole thing in order to show the disciples his glory. In Luke's telling of the story he seems to suggest that such a transfiguration could also happen to the readers too, when they pray.

3. *The teaching on prayer*

At the end of Chapter 10 and the beginning of Chapter 11 there is an interesting Lukan directive on prayer. Typically, Luke gives the reader vivid anecdotes rather than rules.

He tells the story of Martha and Mary and then adds a humorous parable about the nagging friend. Prayer, says Luke, is a lifeline between heaven and earth. It is present when people passively listen to God (Mary) and also when they ask God for their needs (the friend).

Both aspects, listening and asking, are illustrated in the prayer which stands between the two stories (Luke 11:2–4). Only Luke introduces this shorter and simpler (probably older) version of the Lord's Prayer, with a glimpse of Jesus himself at prayer.

### Luke and the Spirit

Jesus on his knees, says Luke, is Jesus opening himself to the Spirit. Those who read the Gospel with the Holy Spirit in mind will see the numerous references to the Spirit. In the infancy narrative the Spirit is mentioned no less than seven times.

For Luke, the Spirit is the way of speaking about the *power* of God at work in the world. This power of God is seen most dramatically in the life and death of Jesus. Christians believe the same Godly Spirit is present in the group of Jesus' disciples.

### Luke and joy

> 'I am here with good news for you, which will bring great joy to all the people.'
>
> (Luke 2:10)

Luke's is the happiest of Gospels. Where Mark had seized on the *fear* which Jesus inspired in people, Luke changes it into *joy*. Perhaps writing twenty years later made all the difference.

1. *The infancy canticles* (songs)
The Good News is already present in the infancy of Jesus. So the people in Luke's story can't contain themselves for joy. The narrative is full of canticles, e.g.

Magnificat (1:46–55)
Benedictus (1:68–79)
Nunc Dimittis (2:29–32)

This note of joy is sustained throughout the Gospel, where every miracle is greeted with joy and praise.

2. *The Good News*
> 'The seventy-two men came back in great joy. "Lord," they said, "even the demons obeyed us when we gave them a command in your name!"'
> (10:17)
> 'The angels of God rejoice over one sinner who repents.' (15:10)
> 'We had to celebrate and be happy, because your brother was dead, but now is alive.' (15:32)

3. *The end of the story*
It is interesting to compare Luke's ending with Mark's. The latter ends on a note of fear.

> *So they went out and ran from the tomb, distressed and terrified. They said nothing to anyone, because they were afraid.*
>
> (Mark 16:8)

But Luke writes:

> *They worshipped him and went back into Jerusalem, filled with great joy, and spent all their time in the Temple giving thanks to God.*
>
> (Luke 24:52–3)

4. *Luke and Paul*
Luke owed much to Paul: his universal outlook and his love for the outsider; but not least his great joy in the Good News.

## Further Issues

Two of Luke's favourite themes need examining a little more closely: God's attitude to the sinner and God's attitude to the poor.

### 1. God's attitude to the sinner

Luke is saying throughout his Gospel that God is revealed to the world in the life and death of Jesus of Nazareth. Look at Jesus and you will see what God is like.

There are various responses that God could make to sin. It is worth considering them.

(a) God could react by exploding with anger. He could be outraged to have his plans upset, his rule disobeyed. He could respond in his anger by taking revenge and striking the sinner down.

(b) God could respond with a controlled rage. He could demand justice in a cool way. Satisfaction must be made, and strictly made, to compensate for the harm that has been done.

(c) God could be far less severe. He could be generous and not ask for justice. He could forgive the sinner without demanding any compensation. He could ask only for repentance, for the promise that the offence will never be committed again.

(d) God could be completely undemanding. His forgiveness could be so total and freely given that no conditions whatsoever are attached. In fact, God could act towards the sinner as if he had not sinned. God's attitude wouldn't even change if the sinner repeats his wrongdoing.

Rembrandt's 'Prodigal Son'

Forgiveness of sin is one of the key Christian doctrines. What do Christians believe about the forgiveness of sin? Which of the four responses do they think God makes? It may help you to decide if you read what Luke has to say about it.

| | *God's attitude towards the sinner* |
|---|---|
| Luke 5:29–32 | Jesus was most at home with the outcasts of society. |
| Luke 6:27–38 | Jesus suggests that our attitude to sinners should be one of *total* forgiveness. |
| Luke 6:36 | Compare this verse with Matthew 5:48. Matthew says be *perfect* like God. Luke says be *merciful* like God. |
| Luke 7:36–50 | Notice how Simon rejects a sinner, but Jesus sees beyond the sin and accepts the person. He recognizes Mary's love. Simon couldn't see it. |
| Luke 9:51–6 | Jesus rebuked James and John for being unforgiving. |
| Luke 11:2–4 | Jesus presumes that we forgive others. Verse 4 is a reference to Deuteronomy 15:1 |
| Luke 15 | These three parables tell of God's joy in accepting sinners. In the parable of the Prodigal Son, God is lavish in his acceptance. |
| Luke 19:1–10 | Zacchaeus reformed because of Jesus' welcome. |
| Luke 23:32–49 | Jesus forgave his persecutors. Christians look at Jesus on the cross and say, 'That is how God is.' |

Luke is making it really quite clear that Jesus was preaching about a God who grants people a totally free pardon from sin. In fact, Luke was saying that Jesus' own life manifested the total forgiveness of a loving God. Luke opts, then for response (d). How many people are as forgiving as this?

When Christians are asked which of these four responses they think God makes, it is surprising how many will settle for (b) or (c). The absoluteness of the fourth response is really too frightening to contemplate, and at the same time too good to be true.

Luke is anxious that his readers get the message: people are not forgiven because they have repented, or because they have believed, or because they have earned it or because they are good. They are forgiven, whatever they are like, because God is good. And that says Luke, is cause for great joy.

## 2. God's attitude to the poor

God's concern for the poor is so dear to Luke that he cannot restrain himself from returning repeatedly to this theme. Luke praises poverty because that condition puts people in the best position to need God and therefore to be open to him. It's the 'have-nots' who are the lucky ones Jesus and Luke turn everything upside down.

It has already been noted on page 26 that Luke is taking up an Old Testament theme of the *anawim*, God's poor.

*Poverty in the Old Testament*

When God first revealed his name to Moses it was as the one who was distressed by his people's misery.

> *I know all about their sufferings, and so I have come down to rescue them.* (Exodus 3:8)

The psalms speak of God as the one who is concerned for the helpless and weak. In Psalm 82 God addresses people of power with these words:

> *You must stop judging unjustly;*
> *you must be no longer partial to the wicked!*
> *Defend the rights of the poor and the orphans;*
> *be fair to the needy and the helpless.* (Psalm 82: 2–3)

The theme runs through the Old Testament, where God is seen as the one who *'rescues the oppressed from the power of evil men'*. (Jeremiah 20:13)

*Jesus the Poor Man*

That rescue came with Jesus, says Luke. Jesus is the poor man, the humble man who sought with the crowd the baptism of repentance (Luke 3:21). Jesus knew hunger (4:3–4), he knew powerlessness (4:5–8) and he put all his trust in God. Born in a borrowed manger and buried in a borrowed tomb, Jesus was the perfect expression of the biblical poor man. Rembrandt captures the simplicity and humanity of Jesus in the charming pen drawing of 'The Holy Family Asleep'.

*Three key texts in Luke*

(a)  In Luke's Gospel Jesus begins his preaching by quoting from Isaiah:

*The Spirit of the Lord is upon me,*
*because he has chosen me to bring*
*good news to the poor.*
*He has sent me to proclaim liberty to*
*the captives,*
*and recovery of sight to the blind;*
*to set free the oppressed*
*and announce that the time has come*
*when the Lord will save his people.*

Luke 4:18–19
cf Isaiah 61:1–2

In the pages of the Gospel that follow, Jesus in his preaching and in his actions sets people free, restores their sight and offers them the Good News.

There are the outcasts who are accepted
(Luke  5:27–8;  7:1–10;  7:36–50;  10:25–37;  17:16–19; 19:1–10)
There are the sick who are healed
(Luke 4:33–7; 4:40; 6:6–10; 7:21; 9:38–43; 13:10–13)
There are the sinners who are welcomed
(Luke 7:36–50; Chapter 15; 17:4; 23:43)

Jesus was at home with a strange assortment of people: tax collectors, fishermen, Samaritans, Roman centurions, lepers, possessed (mad) people and sinners.

An Indian shoeshine boy—
outcast of society in this
sergeant's eyes

When John's disciples ask for a sign from Jesus that he is the one expected, Jesus answers by quoting again from Isaiah:

> The blind can see, the lame can walk, those who suffer from dreaded skin-diseases are made clean, the deaf can hear, the dead are raised to life and the Good News is preached to the poor.
>
> Luke 7: 22–3    cf Isaiah 35: 5–6

(b) Happiness and poverty go hand in hand. Luke is fascinated by this teaching of Jesus.

> Happy are you poor;
> the Kingdom of God is yours!
> Happy are you who are hungry now;
> you will be filled!
> Happy are you who weep now;
> you will laugh!
> Happy are you when people hate you, reject you, insult you, and say that you are evil, all because of the Son of Man! Be glad when this happens, and dance for joy, because a great reward is kept for you in heaven. For their ancestors did the very same things to the prophets.
>
> Luke 6:20–23

These 'bombshell' statements (Barclay's word) are known as the Beatitudes. It is interesting to note how the infancy narrative is almost a meditation on this exact theme. Elizabeth, Zechariah, Mary, the shepherds, Simeon and Anna are all poor people. They all come to know great joy, because in their poverty they turn to God who fills their emptiness.

Luke matches his four beatitudes with four woes.

> But how terrible for you who are rich now;
> you have had your easy life!
> How terrible for you who are full now;
> you will go hungry!
> How terrible for you who laugh now;
> you will mourn and weep!
> How terrible when all people speak well of you; their ancestors said the very same things about the false prophets.
>
> Luke 6:24–6

It is terrible for these rich people because having all they want they don't feel the need for anything else. The rich so easily become the proud (Luke 1:51), and the unrepentant (3:7–9). They are the priest and the Levite in the parable of the Good Samaritan (Luke 10:31–?). In many Lukan parables the rich man misses out (Luke 16:19–31; 18:9–14). When the rich man wanted to follow Jesus but couldn't bring himself to make the sacrifice, Luke tells us that Jesus said: 'How hard it is for rich people to enter the Kingdom of God' (Luke 18:24). And it is Luke alone who has the long section of the right use of money in Chapter 16.

(c) The Jews spoke in the Old Testament of the golden age when God would break into history. They called it the Day of the Lord and they often spoke of it in terms of a banquet.

> Here on Mount Zion the Lord Almighty will prepare a banquet for all the nations of the world—a banquet of the richest food and the finest wine.
>
> Isaiah 25:6

Luke takes up this theme very readily, for as John Drury remarks in his commentary on Luke, this writer has a definite middle-class background and is at home with people who often entertain.

It isn't surprising that Luke develops the suggestion of the Psalmist that it is the poor who are the guests at the feast.

*The poor will eat as much as they want;*
*those who come to the Lord will praise him.*

Psalm 22:26

Chapter 14 of Luke is set around a meal. During this meal Jesus tells his host:

*When you give a feast, invite the poor, the crippled, the lame, and the blind*

Luke 14:13

It is at this meal that Jesus tells the parable of the Wedding Feast and the parable of the Great Feast. In the former he emphasizes that the mighty are put down from their seats whilst the humble are honoured. In the latter the invitation is rejected by those first called to the Kingdom of God and so is offered to the poor, the crippled, the blind and the lame.

When reading through Luke's Gospel notice how often Jesus is at meals or speaks about them. Three times he is accused of eating with sinners (Luke 5:30; 7:39; 15:3). He talks of Gentiles coming to sit down at the feast in the Kingdom of God (Luke 13:29). Jesus invites himself to dine with Zacchaeus, the hated tax collector (Luke 19:1–10). A feast is prepared for the lost son (Luke 15:11–32). Lazarus, the poor man (Luke 16:20–22), is the one who feasts with Abraham. It is to be totally expected that Luke presents the risen Jesus meeting his disciples at a meal (Luke 24:13–35).

*Conclusion*
Luke of all the four gospel writers sees that there is no limit to the love of God. He seems completely in tune with the compassion of Jesus. He is, in Dante's phrase, *'the faithful recorder of Christ's loving kindness'*.

Food for today's poor

## A  Quick answers on the text.

1.  Who are the Gentiles?
2.  Why is it significant that Luke traces the ancestry of Jesus back to *Adam*?
3.  Name four women mentioned by Luke in his Gospel.
4.  Why (according to Luke) did Jesus go up the mountain where he was transfigured?
5.  Name the Old Testament characters who appeared to Jesus when he was transfigured.
6.  Mark's Gospel ends on a note of fear. On what note does Luke's Gospel end?
7.  Luke was influenced by the first Christian missionary. Who was he?
8.  What does the word *anawim* mean?
9.  In Jesus' 'Beatitudes' what is promised to the poor?
10.  How many 'Beatitudes' does Matthew mention? How many does Luke mention?
11.  Give two instances where Luke shows Jesus at prayer.
12.  Luke likes meals. Give two examples from the Gospel where a meal is at the centre of the scene.

## B  Longer answers

1.  Show, by close reference to the Gospel that Luke makes special reference to Samaritans.
2.  Describe an incident in Luke's Gospel where Jesus helped someone who was not a Jew.
3.  Give some examples of three characteristic features of Luke's Gospel.
4.  List the many groups of people who were considered as 'outsiders'.

## C  Essays

1.  You have been asked to talk to a group of people about Luke's Gospel. They have never read it. What main points would you make to show them what is typical of Luke's Gospel? Illustrate your answer by referring to selected passages from the Gospel.

2.  Describe *two* incidents in Luke's Gospel in which a woman is prominent. What is Luke telling us about Jesus in each case?
3.  How does Luke's Gospel give a prominent place to prayer? Illustrate your answer by referring to selected passages.
4.  'To be forgiven completely is probably more difficult than to forgive.' Discuss.
5.  It is said that Matthew's eight Beatitudes say nothing different from Luke's four. Do you agree? (Matthew 5:3–12 and Luke 6:20–23)
6.  'The poor baby in a stable, recognized by poor people, is already a summary of the whole of Luke's Gospel.' Comment.

## D  For individuals and groups to do

1.  Make a frieze illustrating the characteristics of Luke's Gospel, using the headings from the text to guide you.
2.  Make up an anthology of modern poetry and prose which ties in, in some way, with what you have understood of Luke. (Give Gospel references to make the connections clear.)
3.  Read again the story of the transfiguration (Luke 9:28ff). Then turn to pages 43 and 115 and look at the way the two icon painters have interpreted the story. Make a few comments.

G

# B10  Who was Jesus?

*Jesus Christ, Superstar,*
*tell us that you're who they say you are. . . .*
*Jesus Christ, Superstar,*
*Do you think you're what they say you are?*

The popular Webber-Rice rock opera, 'Jesus Christ, Superstar' (first performed in 1970) poses an important question. In the long run, who *was* Jesus? Who did people think he was? Would he have agreed?

### Whom do men say?

The gospel writers themselves are aware that this is an important question. All four of them present a scene in which Jesus asks, *'Who do people think I am? Who do* you *think I am?* In all four Gospels, his disciples devoutly acknowledge that he is the *'Holy One of God'*, the *'Christ of God'* (See Luke 9:20). And Jesus seems to accept the compliment.

There is of course a difficulty here, which any thoughtful reader will spot. The Gospels tell us clearly enough who the authors (and the community they were writing for) thought Jesus was. But how can we tell whether in actual fact Jesus himself would have agreed with this description of himself?

The short answer is that we can't tell. The Gospels never claimed to be biographies of Jesus, telling us simply who Jesus *was*. They claim to be something far more valuable, a declaration of who Jesus *is* for the writer.

### Titles

For the writers of the Gospels, Jesus is:

(a) *Messiah* (Hebrew) or *Christ* (Greek)

The word means one 'anointed' (chrismed) by God, that is, chosen out for a special task. The Old Testament gives this title to all the Israelite kings. When kings were no more, the title referred (and for many Jews still does) to the hoped-for future king who would restore the glory of Israel, and bring peace and prosperity to the whole world. The New Testament gives the title to Jesus so readily that it becomes almost his surname. 'Jesus, the Christ' becomes simply 'Jesus Christ'.

(b) *Son of God*

This is a closely-related title, also given to the kings of Israel, who thought of themselves as visible stand-ins for the invisible God. Israel's ruler was enthroned, like a son, at the 'right hand' of the real ruler, God. The royal palace in Jerusalem was at the right hand (south) of the Temple (See Psalms 2 and 110). Jesus is referred to as Son of God throughout the four Gospels. To ask, *'Are you the Son of God?'* (Luke 22:70) means the same as, *'Are you the Christ?'* (Luke 22:67).

(c) *Servant of God*

This is another related title; as Son of God, the king and his people must above all obey God's will. But it has overtones of suffering rather than glory. The book of Isaiah (Chapters 42–53) has four magnificent poems about the ideal Israel as a servant, undergoing pain and persecution in order to fulfil its role, but finally being vindicated by God and exalted in glory. The New Testament sees Jesus as fitting that description perfectly. He is the ideal Israel, even though he has to suffer to claim that title (See Luke 22:27).

### (d) *Son of Man*

Paradoxically, this title has far stronger supernatural overtones than the royal title 'Son of God'. The book of Daniel (7:13) had used it as a symbol of a humane Israel, which would one day replace all the bestial empires which the world had so far known. Later writers made this symbol into an individual person, scarcely distinguishable from God himself. This person, they hoped, would eventually descend from heaven to announce Kingdom Come. The Gospels often speak as if Jesus regularly used this title of himself, and with these supernatural overtones (See Luke 12:8; 12:40; 17:24; 21:27; 22:69).

### (e) *Lord*

The Greek word *kyrios* (lord) has many meanings. At its lowest it can be translated simply as 'sir', and was used as a courtesy title of any superior. At its highest it was the word used to translate the Old Testament name of God himself, Yahweh or Jehovah. This title was given to Jesus after the resurrection, and with such a high meaning that it became a profession of faith ('Jesus is Lord'). But the gospel writers, especially Luke, easily give Jesus that title even before the resurrection (See Luke 2:11; 5:8; 7:6; 9:54; 10:1; 11:1; 12:41, etc.).

### Fair comment

The section above tells us clearly and forcefully what the New Testament authors thought about Jesus. For them he was the divinely appointed Messiah-Christ, the royal Son of God, the ideal Suffering Servant, the heavenly Son of Man, the divine Lord in person. It does not, of course, tell us who Jesus *actually* was, or what he thought of himself.

It can safely be presumed that these titles were 'fair comment' on the sort of person Jesus actually was. His disciples would hardly have given such highflown titles to someone who in no way fitted them. What they had seen and heard and experienced of Jesus drove them to describe him in these superlative terms.

But there is no evidence that Jesus himself ever claimed these titles or these descriptions of himself. In fact all the evidence is in the opposite direction. All the titles, especially the title of Messiah-Christ, had such misleading overtones, that he was reluctant to claim them. He seems at times even to have repudiated them (See Luke 9:21; 22:70).

The fact is, while his followers were later anxious to preach about him, he himself had only been anxious to preach about the Kingdom or Rule of God his Father. If he did use the words 'Son of Man' about himself (and this seems likely), it would have been in a very low key, meaning no more than 'I myself'.

### Jesus lost forever

Does this mean that we know nothing of Jesus himself? That he has been forever lost behind the enthusiastic interpretation of his disciples? Not at all. From behind the interpretations, a most powerful, impressive, challenging, indeed unique personality still emerges. Here is what a modern and highly critical New Testament scholar says is the inescapable truth about Jesus:

*Jesus had certain attitudes and standards—he demanded honour, goodness, consecration, unselfishness and love—what he called 'perfection'—from everyone, and he would settle for nothing less... But yet, he welcomed people into his company and full friendship without their having come anywhere near meeting his demands. He freely gave his friendship to extortionists and prostitutes and all sorts of people who were nowhere near having attained the perfection he demanded. He called people to come and stand beside him, to adopt his relationship and attitude to others. They were to come without any pretence of having attained perfection: and yet without any fear of being rejected by Jesus... And all this he did in God's name. His attitude he said is God's attitude and if men have accepted his call and entered into relationship with him, then they are in that same relationship with God...*

*This means that as he saw it, people's relationship with God was essentially bound up with their relationship to him. To 'follow' Jesus, to accept his call and forgiving friendship is to partake in God's Kingdom, to be in the true relationship to God. Therefore Jesus believed that with his appearance the time of salvation had arrived... Jesus' aim was not so much to introduce a new concept of God but to open for men a new relationship with God, a relationship which means certainty of being accepted, and so freedom from anxiety, and thus sonship, liberty, simplicity, love.*

D. Nineham *The New Testament Gospels* (B.B.C., 1965.)

It is no wonder that those who first heard this liberating message gave its preacher superhuman titles.

### God or man?

To conclude, when Christians are asked, 'Who was Jesus?', they will tend to give one of two answers. Some will state that Jesus is 'God' without further qualification. His humanity was nothing more than a temporary disguise for what he really was. They accept the supernatural language of the Gospels quite literally and uncritically, because this language speaks to them. They take as their starting point the stories of his virgin birth, his miraculous powers, his resurrection from the dead and his ascension into heaven. These are precisely the stories one would expect of a God visiting the earth.

Others wish to take the humanity of Jesus far more seriously. They take as their starting point the man Jesus who gave rise to such remarkable stories. They want to respect the stories as powerful expressions of what Jesus means to the believer, but do not find it necessary to take the stories literally. For them, Jesus was a man like the rest of men, limited by every human limitation. What set him apart from the rest of men was his closeness to God. He was so at one with God that those who were close to him knew they were in the presence of God. And they knew of no other man of whom that could be said.

Both sorts of Christians claim that in Jesus the distinction people usually make—'either God or man'—has been obliterated. In his case the words no longer exclude each other, and perhaps never should have done. The God whom people think of as distant is shown to be close at hand. The mystery that lies at the heart of our world which we call God—is revealed in the most ordinary thing, the life of a man.

All readers of the Gospel are invited to make their own decision about Jesus.

Part C

# Luke for Today

# C1 Introduction

Luke addresses his Gospel and the Acts of the Apostles to Theophilus. This could be an important official. But Theophilus means 'God-lover' and so it could be that he addresses his work to all people who love God. That is how Christians see it.

Christians believe that the Gospel is for all time. They believe that the Kingdom of God came with the life of Jesus, and they believe that the Kingdom of God is still present in the world.

If you look at a daily newspaper you may well ask the question 'Where is this Kingdom of God supposed to be?' Our newspapers carry daily reports on wars, worries and woes. According to Luke the Good News of God's Kingdom is to do with peace, freedom from anxiety and joy.

This section is a kind of anthology, a collage of ideas. It is intended as a jumping-off point for discussions, group work or projects.

The world today is complex. As the industrial nations use up the world's resources, they create as many problems as they solve. The gap between rich and poor nations widens daily. The arms race causes worldwide alarm. Industrial nations replace people with machines to create wealth. Unemployment is the result. Poor nations have no machines to create jobs. Unemployment is the result. Crime increases with the frustration this produces. Medicine improves, people live longer and the population problem is increased. Wars go on day by day. Many of them are the result of religious fervour and intolerance.

What have the Christian churches to say about a world like this? One thing is quite clear. There are no easy answers. There are Christians who stand, firmly convinced, on both sides of most arguments. It is not possible to look in the Gospels for all the answers to today's problems. Many of the problems didn't exist in the time of Jesus. What does the Christian do? Obviously, anyone who takes Jesus seriously cannot remain apathetic and unconcerned about the world. A Christian is someone who does ask questions. Christians usually look to their church for guidance, but ultimately they make up their own minds in interpreting today's world in the light of the Gospel. Jesus, himself, never stopped asking questions and some of the answers he came up with contradicted the Jewish Law.

In the following notes it will become clear that today's Christians can also get into conflict with authority, even in a so-called Christian society. Being a Christian is not always comfortable.

# C2 Rich and poor

### Some facts

A nun who shares her life with the poor in Peru

The root cause of worldwide hostilities is the uneven distribution of wealth. The world can be divided up in different ways. One way is the description of a First, Second and Third world. The First World is the rich countries of North America, Europe, Japan, Australia and New Zealand. The Second World is the Eastern bloc—East Europe and the Soviet Union. The Third World is the countries of Central and S. America, Africa, most of Asia and the Pacific Islands. Most of the world's poor and hungry people are in the Third World. They also have the largest population. (They could be called the Two-thirds World!) More recently the world has been divided into the rich North and the poor South.

The Gospel puts before Christians the dangers of possessing wealth.

> *No servant can be the slave of two masters; he will hate the one and love the other; he will be loyal to one and despise the other. You cannot serve both God and money.*
>
> Luke 16:13

Individuals have always found it possible to share their possessions. In Luke's second volume he describes how the early followers of Jesus shared all they had:

> *The group of believers was one in mind and heart. No one said that any of his belongings was his own, but they all shared with one another everthing they had... There was no one in the group who was in need.*
>
> Acts 4:32, 34

### Ask yourself

- It has been suggested that the European Economic Community was formed to strengthen the participating countries *against* others. What do you think?
- Does it seem to you that Christians take a lead in working for the poor?
- The Communist ideal states *'From everyone according to his capacity, to everyone according to his need.'* In what way is this different from the ideal of the early Christian community?

Lunch in a children's house on a kibbutz

*'Happy are you poor: the Kingdom of God is yours.'*

Luke 6:20

A starving Ethiopian girl mourns her dead brother

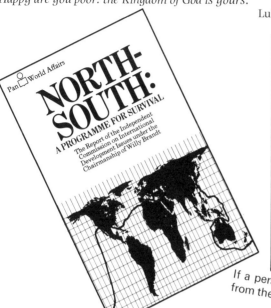

If a person is in extreme necessity, he has the right to take from the riches of others what he, himself, needs.
*The Church in the Modern World, n.69 Vatican II*

In 1974 Henry Kissinger said to the World Food Conference:

*... within a decade no child will go to bed hungry ... no family will fear for its next day's bread and no human being's future and capacity will be stunted by malnutrition.*

**What went wrong?** The ten years have come and gone, and 40,000 children *die* every day from hunger and its related diseases. 500,000,000 people still go hungry every day.

Hungry children in a Colombian shanty town with only sacks for clothing

**Q** It is very hard to get my church to support Christian Aid. When I talked to my minister about it last week he said he thought feeding people's minds was more important than feeding their bodies.

**A** We tend to think of feeding bodies and feeding minds as two very different things. But God created people as whole human beings. Bodies and minds cannot be completely separated.

Christian Aid does not simply feed people's bodies. We are concerned about them as people. We believe that God does not want people to go hungry or to suffer injustice. If Christians are not helping the poor there is something seriously wrong.

*The world's population is likely to double within our life-time.*

A politician in the 1950s said that television would enable us to sit at home and watch each other starve.

*A community which has no synagogue and no shelter for the poor, must first provide for the poor.*
Sefer Chasidim

A refugee camp for the homeless

# C3  Poverty in Britain

An old person in need of help

### Some facts

Here in Britain we belong to one of the wealthy nations of the world, but we still have a poverty problem. On a visit to London, Mother Teresa of Calcutta pointed out that we have a different kind of poverty—a poverty of loneliness. It is a poverty of spirit.

The problem of old age, alcoholism and drug addiction are all 'diseases' of developed nations like Britain. Can you say why?

*Happy are you poor;*
*the Kingdom of God is yours.*

Luke 6:20

How can this Beatitude give hope to today's poor? Christians certainly don't praise poverty for its own sake. It is *not* a good thing to be poor because it brings suffering, deprivation; it inhibits people, it prevents them from being fully human. Christians have always tried to alleviate poverty. They are often in the forefront of campaigns to better the living conditions of the poor.

But whatever misery poverty can cause, it can also make people aware of their need. This, Luke's Gospel says, is reason to be glad about poverty.

### Ask yourself

- Why are more young people today turning to alcohol? What do you know about 'Alcoholics Anonymous' and the 'Samaritans'?
- An entirely new approach to work and leisure is demanded in the developed nations. Have you any suggestions about what could be done?
- Do you think more money always brings more happiness?
- Some poor people in the Third World feel quite sorry for us—the rich people of the First World. Can you think why?

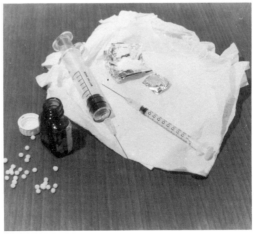

*Streets of London*

*Have you seen the old man*
*In the closed down market*
*Kicking up the papers with his worn-out shoes?*
*In his eyes you see no pride*
*Hands held loosely by his side*
*Yesterday's paper, telling yesterday's news.*

*So how can you tell me you're lonely*
*And say for you that the sun don't shine?*
*Let me take you by the hand*
*And lead you through the streets of London*
*I'll show you something that'll make you change your mind.*

Ralph McTell

# UNEMPLOYMENT

## Good News about Depression

*Alcoholism*

No use knocking on the window—
Some are lucky, some are not, sir.
We are Christian men and women,
But we're keeping what we've got, sir.

Standing in the rain. . .

# Church justified in closing doors to the homeless

by Peter Stanford

CHURCH bodies have this week reiterated their "very real concern" at the plight of the growing numbers of single homeless in London, but have defended a Westminster diocesan directive advising priests not to open up church ha'' temporary night she' The current DHS' limiting those breakfast eigh'

and housing authorities to evade their responsibilities for meeting people's housing rights", the SPA letter stated.

It has received wid support from the and Catholic London.

## Drug addiction is increasing and the users are younger

By Martin Fletcher

The number of drug offences, addicts and seizures all rose last according to Home Office car. The figures also show the hard drugs is rs are young

to 2,450, 2,500 and 700. The led the number of drugs trafficking specialist drugs investigators offences rose by 24 per cent to announced the formation of t 4,100. National Drugs Unit, pro

Nearly 30 per cent (7,200) of £115 million for local offenders were under the age of and rehabilitation 21 and the number of offenders embarked on under the age of 17 increased by education campaign. 17 per cent to 707. Seizures of drugs rose by 9 cate 1' per cent to 28,560 in 1984, but traff' seizures of soft drugs such his rose by just 5 per of hard dr 'cor

*WARD CLOSURE*

# C4 *People left out*

Bishop Trevor Huddleston

**Some facts**

In every society and group there are people who are pushed aside and left on the fringe. We have seen that in Luke's Gospel Jesus seemed to go out of his way to make the outcasts of society his heroes and heroines. He put them *first*. Following this example, Christians through the ages have worked for the poor and neglected.

Find out what you can about

St Francis of Assisi           Bishop Trevor Huddleston
William Wilberforce         Robert Raikes
Dr Barnardo                      Mother Teresa of Calcutta
St Vincent de Paul           Leonard Cheshire
Father Damien                  Sue Ryder
Albert Schweitzer

But Christians have also been guilty of prejudice and intolerance.

Jewish children also faced
persecution

> Christian whites in South Africa earnestly believed that the Bible showed them to be a superior race. This is the cause of the apartheid system.

> This terrible persecution of the Jews in Germany was the result of centuries of hatred and mistrust by Christian people.

Home is a squatter's camp
for this black South
African child

*'Hurry down Zacchaeus, because I must stay in your house today.'*
*Zacchaeus hurried down and welcomed him with great joy. All the*
*people who saw it started grumbling, 'This man has gone as a guest to*
*the home of a sinner'.*

Luke 19:5–7

Jesus was anxious to show that it is the good actions of people that matter, not the labels they wear. Many people who don't wear the Christian label are very concerned about outcasts. Do you know anyone like this?

**Ask yourself**

- The United Nations proclaimed a Universal Declaration of Human Rights. Find out what you can about it.
- What is it that makes people so easily prejudiced? Fear and ignorance. Can you think of any more reasons?
- What is it that makes people fight their own prejudices and work for the good of others?
- People can be left out and made to feel inferior even in your school group. Talk about it.

# My mugger was in his forties, wearing a suit, collar and tie

ANNA DAVIDSON, a civil servant, was walking through a subway at London's Elephant and Castle one night when she was attacked and robbed.

'It was about 11 p.m. I heard footsteps behind me, but didn't take any notice, even when they began to speed up. Perhaps someone had a train to catch.

The next thing I knew a man jumped right round in front of me and asked me the way to Waterloo. I turned round to give him directions and without any warning he punched me on the side of the jaw.

I was knocked halfway to the ground, but all I could say was, "Don't be stupid." I was so shocked. It was a strange feeling it happening, but at the same time not believing it. I didn't even feel angry with him, I was too stunned.

The other thing was that he looked so normal. It wasn't the terrifying picture of a mugger at all. He was in his forties and wearing an ordinary dark suit, with shirt and tie. That astounded me the fact that someone like this was wearing a collar and tie. The sheer middle-classness of him probably contributed to the shock. I was only 19.

Then he said, "Give us a kiss." I pushed him away, saying, "I want to go home; don't be so stupid." Several things went through my mind. One was that perhaps he had been drinking. Another was that if I struck back he might have a knife or a gun.

Then he knocked me down again. I must have lost consciousness. When I came round he wasn't there, my handbag was gone and I was in a terrible mess. An elderly couple came by, and I yelled out, "Can you help me?", but they walked straight by.

It was a black man and his girlfriend who did stop. They helped me to a telephone box to call for an ambulance.'

AMNESTY INTERNATIONAL

Please review the case of
GRIGORY BERMAN in the light
of elementary justice.

From: Father Patrick O'Mahony,
Our Lady of the Wayside,
Shirley, Warwickshire,
England

To:
The General Secretary
of the Soviet Communist
Party,
The Kremlin,
Moscow, RUSSIA

'Free Mandela' demonstration

A leper

**FEARS**

## Being a Good Samaritan's all right— if you've got the time

**Q** I go to the over 60's Club at our community centre every Tuesday. Last week someone from Christian Aid came and showed us a film. She said we should be helping people in India. It really makes me angry. Why should we? We've got enough problems here. If you tried to live on a pension or supplementary benefit you'd soon find out. Why don't you think more about people here?

**A** If we only look at our own problems we do not get a full picture. Take one example – food. Some of the world's poorest countries are growing tea, coffee, bananas and pineapples for us. Without them, we could not enjoy these things.

They sell their food to us while their own people are too poor to buy it. The prices they get from us have not gone up nearly as much as the prices we charge for the machinery and other things we sell them. It's a small world and we sink or swim together.

Starving children in a Warsaw ghetto

Jesus Christ has gone to heaven,
One day he'll be coming back, sir.
In this house he will be welcome.
But we hope he won't be black, sir.

Standing in the rain...

*"Why should we help people thousands of miles away? What has it got to do with us?"*

# C5 The Gospel and liberation

### Some facts

In recent years many Christians who belong to the Third World, or who work there, have been faced with a problem. How far should they become involved in politics?

There are many Christians who say 'not at all'. They believe that the message of Jesus is an exclusively spiritual one. But there are many others who believe that following Jesus leads them right into political conflict. Jesus' message was not primarily political but his actions and words brought him constantly up against the political powers of his day.

It has been noted already that the *Magnificat* is a revolutionary song.

> *He has stretched out his mighty arm*
> *and scattered the proud with all their plans.*
> *He has brought down mighty kings from their thrones,*
> *and lifted up the lowly.*
>
> Luke 1:51, 52.

In the countries where injustice and poverty crush most of the population it is Christians who are taking a lead in political action to bring about revolution. Some of these Christians believe in non-violent revolution. But some believe that violence may be needed to bring about justice. This is a new and controversial issue in the churches. It is known as 'liberation theology'. It is mostly associated with the Roman Catholic Church in Central and South America.

Two faces of Nicaragua — the new literacy campaign and the Sandinista Popular Guard

### Ask yourself

- Do you believe that aid should be conditional on the political record of a developing country?
- Find out what you can about Che Guevara, Archbishop Romero of San Salvador, Fr Leonardo Boff and Bishop Helder Camara of Brazil.
- What would be the arguments *for* and *against* liberation theology?
- There are those who would say that the I.R.A. are religious freedom fighters and therefore their actions are justified. What do you think?

*I call out in the night from the torture chamber*

Psalm 129

*From the depth I call to you Lord*
*I call out in the night from prison*
*from the concentration camp*
*From the torture chamber*
*in the hour of darkness*
*hear my voice*
*my S.O.S.*

*If you draw up the record of sins*
*Lord who would have a clean slate?*
*But you pardon sins*
*you are not implacable like them in their*
*investigations*

*I trust in the Lord and not in the leaders*
*Not in slogans*
*I trust in the Lord and not in their radios!*

*My soul hopes in the Lord*
*more than guards watching for dawn*
*more than prisoners counting the night hours*

*We are jailed*
*while they are partying*
*But the Lord is liberation*
*freedom for Israel*

Ernesto Cardenal of Nicaragua
*Psalms of Struggle and Liberation*

A victim of the Vietnamese War

Central America

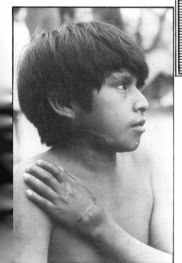

Scarred for life with machete
wounds, El Salvador

*When will the Churches—even if*
*they run the risk of moving out from*
*the religious field to invade the*
*territory of politics—decide to*
*denounce injustices from whatever*
*system they arise, in the secure con-*
*viction that without justice there*
*will be no peace?*
Archbishop Helder Camara
speaking in Liverpool

Dear Mr President:

A recent news item in the press has concerned me very much. According to the article, your administration is studying the possibility of backing the present government junta and giving it economic and military aid. Because you are Christian and have said that you want to defend human rights, I take the liberty of expressing my pastoral point of view on this matter and of making a specific request.

I am deeply disturbed over the news that the United States government is studying a way to accelerate El Salvador's arms race by sending military teams and advisers to "instruct three of El Salvador's batallions in logistics, communications and intelligence techniques". If this information is true, the contribution of your administration, instead of favouring greater justice and peace in El Salvador, will almost surely intensify the injustice and repression of the common people who are organized to struggle for respect for their most basic human rights. Since I as a Salvadoran and archbishop of the San Salvador archdiocese have the obligation to work for the reign of faith and justice in my country, I urge you, if you really want to defend human rights
☐ to prohibit the giving of military assistance to the Salvadoran government
☐ to guarantee that your government will not intervene directly or indirectly with military, economic, diplomatic or other pressure to determine the fate of the Salvadoran people.

It would be deplorable and unjust if by the intervention of foreign powers the Salvadoran people should be frustrated, repressed and hindered from deciding autonomously the economic and political course our country should follow.

It would mean violating a right that we Latin American bishops meeting in Puebla publicly acknowledged—"Legitimate self-determination for our peoples. This will permit them to organize their lives in accordance with their own genius and history and to cooperate in a new international order".

I hope your religious sentiments and your sensitivity for the defense of human rights will move you to accept my request and thereby avoid greater bloodshed in this long-suffering country.

Sincerely, **Oscar A Romero**, Archbishop, February 17, 1980.

*One month later Archbishop Romero*
*was shot while saying mass.*

# C6 War and peace

### Some facts

*'I can go into my office, pick up the telephone and in 25 minutes 70 million people will be dead.'* These words of the American ex-president, Richard Nixon, show the enormity of the nuclear threat of war.

At any given time there is a war being fought somewhere in the world. People are always wanting to exert power over others.

> *But the people there would not receive him. . . When the disciples James and John saw this, they said, 'Lord, do you want us to call fire down from heaven to destroy them?' Jesus turned and rebuked them.*
>
> Luke 9:53–5

James and John thought Jesus would approve of their proposal to destroy the 'enemy'. They wanted revenge. Jesus rebuked them for it. His way was that of forgiveness and peace.

There are many Christians who believe that this sets the standard for all human behaviour in regard to war. They are *pacifists*, who refuse to take military action against others.

The Christian churches, themselves, have not taken this extreme line. They have always claimed that there can be a 'just war'.

But the nuclear build-up of arms has introduced grave problems into the question of when a war is justified.

> *Nuclear weapons are an offence to God and a denial of his purpose for man. Only the reduction of these weapons and their eventual abolition can remove this offence. No other policy can be acceptable to Christian conscience.*
>
> British Council of Churches.

Mahatma Gandhi

### Ask yourself

- Is God on anyone's side in a war?
- What is multilateral disarmament, and what is unilateral disarmament? How is it that prominent Christians speak out on both sides of the nuclear disarmament debate?
- 'If we take an eye for an eye soon the whole world will be blind.' (Mahatma Gandhi) Think about these words.

War as a method of settling international disputes is incompatible with the teaching and example of Our Lord Jesus Christ.

LAMBETH 1930, 1948, 1958, 1968, 1978.

*Modern weapons of war are evidence of madness. Society is spending its best brains and much of its budget on planning the* lunatic unthinkable.

Dr. Robert Runcie, (B.B.C., November 1980)

Few Christians take non-violence seriously. Despite the heroic examples of such men as Jesus Christ, Martin Luther King, Danilo Dolci and Archbishop Helder Camara, non-violence has hardly had a look-in on the thinking within the Church, past or present. We praise such men: shouldn't we take them seriously for a change?

Robin Percival

A CND demonstration

## Cheshire V.C.

Group Captain Leonard Cheshire, VC, the wartime bomber pilot who was an eyewitness to the atomic devastation of Nagasaki, is convinced that the nuclear deterrent will prevent a third world war.

**PROTEST**

*Governments cannot be denied the right to legitimate defence once every means of peaceful settlement has been exhausted.*

R.C. document *Church in the Modern World*

**The Nuclear Arsenals**

Monsignor Bruce Kent of CND

### If he asks for bread will you give him bombs?

These words become charged with an even stronger note of warning when we think what is happening. Instead of bread and cultural aids, the new States and nations are being offered modern weapons and means of destruction, and often in abundance. These weapons, the instruments of armed conflicts and wars, are provided less as a requirement for defending just rights and sovereignty than a form of chauvinism, imperialism and neo-colonialism of one kind or another.

We all know well that the areas of misery and hunger on our globe could have been made fertile in a short time, if the gigantic investments for armaments at the service of war and destruction had been changed into investments for food, that is, the service of life.

Pope John Paul II

H

# C7 Family life

## Some facts

The pattern of family life for most people in Britain has been set by two major influences.

(a) *Christianity*. Underlying family life is the Christian teaching on *monogamy*—a secure relationship between one man and one woman for life. The Christian ideal is that this relationship reflects the loving relationship between God and the world.

(b) *The Industrial Revolution*. This development of Britain into an industrial nation brought financial independence for young people, and with it the freedom to choose the marriage partner.

The rapidly changing social and economic patterns of life today place considerable strain on marriage relationships and on the family. Christians look to the Gospel for guidance on moral questions. The guidelines they seek are not always clear cut. The life of Jesus at Nazareth, recorded by Luke, is taken as *the* example of loving, stable relationships within a family.

> *So Jesus went back with them to Nazareth, where he was obedient to them.*
>
> Luke 2:51

Jesus' teaching on divorce is taken by all Christians as an indication that everything should be done to uphold the importance of marriage.

> *Any man who divorces his wife and marries another woman commits adultery; and the man who marries a divorced woman commits adultery.*
>
> Luke 16:18

However, in practice, this Gospel passage is interpreted in different ways within the Christian Church.

1. The Roman Catholic Church does not allow divorce or remarriage at all.

2. Until recently the Church of England allowed divorce but not remarriage. This is now changing.

3. The Orthodox Church does allow remarriage after careful consideration of individual cases.

## Ask yourself

- What social and economic changes in Britain are putting strains on family life?
- 'The roles of parents are changing. Family life itself may not survive.' What do you think about that?
- 'It's selfish and stupid to have large families today.' Is it?
- What moral questions are raised by test-tube babies and surrogate motherhood?

*Marriage is like a three-speed gearbox: affection, friendship, love. It is not advisable to crash your gears and go right through to love straight away.*

Peter Ustinov

---

*A married couple are well suited when both partners usually feel the need for a quarrel at the same time.*

Jean Rostard, *Le Mariage*, 1927

---

*Each one of an affectionate couple may be willing, as we say, to die for the other, yet unwilling to utter the agreeable word at the right moment.*

Meredith, On the Idea of Comedy, 1877

---

*Allow children to be happy in their own way, for what better way will they ever find?*

Dr Johnson, 1780

---

*Don't limit a child to your own learning, for he was born in another time.*

Rabbinic saying

# Abortion couples haunted by grief

**By JOHN ILLMAN**
**Medical Correspondent**

ABORTION can explode in grief and horror for couples as long as ten years after the event, according to a leading specialist.

And Miss Janet Mattinson says that fathers of aborted babies are sometimes more haunted by shame and regret than the mothers.

In a CIBA Foundation book on abortion she pleads with abortion clinics to recognise the ordeal of grieving fathers. She says: 'Fathers would benefit from as much or more attention than women.'

There are many families in Britain today with backgrounds that are not British. Their family patterns are sometimes described in terms of the *extended* family.
What does this mean?
Find out about these other traditions of family life.

## Hermann Gmeiner

was born in Alberschwende, Austria, in 1919 as one of the many children of a Vorarlberg farmer. His mother died when he was young. After the Second World War, he studied medicine at Innsbruck University. He saw the plight of the many homeless children in those post-war years and founded the first SOS Children's Village in Imst, Tyrol. His SOS Idea has since been acclaimed all over the world. Hermann Gmeiner is one of the most prominent as well as the most successful pioneers of child care in a family-like environment. He has received many honors in recognition of his work; he is an honorary member of the Austrian Academy of Sciences and holds honorary doctorates from two universities. "Millions of friends all over the world have helped me to found over 140 SOS Children's Villages", says Hermann Gmeiner. "This is a sensational wave of goodwill! We have realized that the present generation of children must be given the chance to grow up happily if they are to secure a worthwhile future for us all. The reward for our work, our trouble, our sacrifices, is the happy laughter of the twenty thousand children in the SOS Children's Villages all over the world who now have a permanent home and a family of their own."

# C8 Women today

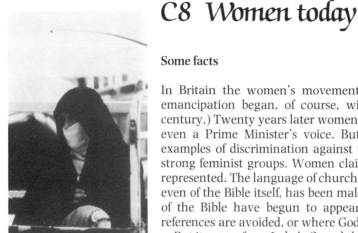
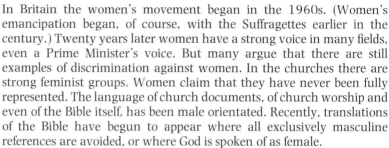

### Some facts

In Britain the women's movement began in the 1960s. (Women's emancipation began, of course, with the Suffragettes earlier in the century.) Twenty years later women have a strong voice in many fields, even a Prime Minister's voice. But many argue that there are still examples of discrimination against women. In the churches there are strong feminist groups. Women claim that they have never been fully represented. The language of church documents, of church worship and even of the Bible itself, has been male orientated. Recently, translations of the Bible have begun to appear where all exclusively masculine references are avoided, or where God is spoken of as female.

But it seems from Luke's Gospel that Jesus himself, was very liberated in his attitude to women. That is to say, he surprised everyone by talking to women and listening to them—and that wasn't 'done' in his society.

> *The twelve disciples went with him, and so did some women... Mary, from whom seven devils had been driven out; Joanna, whose husband Chuza was an officer in Herod's Court; and Suzanna, and many other women who used their own resources to help Jesus and his disciples.*
>
> Luke 8:1–3

Women have been given a different role in different societies.

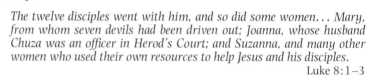

### Ask yourself

- An Arab woman is not expected to act like a British woman. The Islamic tradition gives her a role sometimes described as 'second-class'. Can anyone make a fair judgment from outside?
- In Judaism the *mother* is the central figure in the family and a powerful influence in family life. Find out more about this.
- In Christian South America there is accepted male behaviour called 'machismo'. It means that a proper man is afraid of nobody, is sexually powerful and exercises a tight control over females. A woman is expected to be submissive and to remain at home looking after the family. This female behaviour is sometimes called 'Marianismo', after the mother of Jesus. What do you think about that?
- What are the arguments for and against women priests?
- Why don't Roman Catholic priests marry?

Women today—from the top, Arabian, Jewish, South American

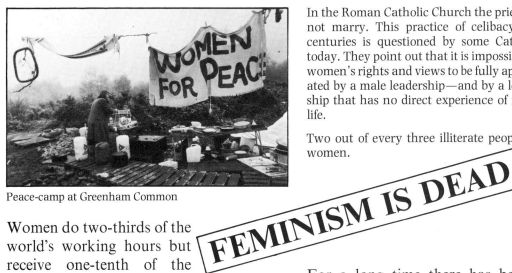

Peace-camp at Greenham Common

In the Roman Catholic Church the priests do not marry. This practice of celibacy over centuries is questioned by some Catholics today. They point out that it is impossible for women's rights and views to be fully appreciated by a male leadership—and by a leadership that has no direct experience of family life.

Two out of every three illiterate people are women.

Women do two-thirds of the world's working hours but receive one-tenth of the income and own one hundredth of the property.

## FEMINISM IS DEAD

Save the Unborn Child
# Life

A woman is supposed to be kind and understanding as a matter of course; if a man is, everyone says that he's amazing

For a long time there has been a Church of England debate on whether to allow women to be ordained priests. The 1985 General Synod voted *for* women to be ordained deacons. There are already ordained ministers in some of the free churches.

Vatican II—a world assembly of the Roman Catholic leaders (1963–65). No women were allowed to vote.

**80% of the men questioned in one survey said that though their wives worked full-time, they expected them to take full responsibility for the household, the shopping and the children**

# C9 Miracles today

A sick Arab refugee girl waits for treatment

## Some facts

The survey reported on pages 30–1 shows that people today still experience 'miracles'. But most of them do not expect their 'miracles' to contradict the laws of nature. Jesus, himself, pointed out that anyone who was open to the love and power of God could do things as wonderful as he did.

> They had come to hear him to be healed of their diseases. Those who were troubled by evil spirits also came and were healed. All the people tried to touch him, for power was going out from him and healing them all.
>
> Luke 6:18–19

*Healing and Health*

Some Christians today claim to have the power of healing. Many fundamentalist preachers (they take the Bible quite literally) claim that they are able to cure people through faith in Jesus. Some even work on American cable television and heal 'across the air'.

Others explain Christian healing in less fundamentalist terms. Michael Wynne Parker, an English healer, points out that the healing of people is primarily a healing of their spirit. '*This must come first. The healing of mind and body naturally follows.*' He emphasizes that Christian healing is the healing of the whole person.

This concern with the healing of the *whole person* is also to be found in today's medical world. Freud, Adler and Jung have made a deep analysis of the psychological element of the human person and of its importance. Many diseases are now called psychosomatic, to indicate how much mind and body affect each other (mind-*psyche*, body-*soma*). These diseases begin in the feeling part of the mind and end in the diseased state of the body.

## Ask yourself

- Find out what you can about psychosomatic diseases.
- How far are doctors and healing ministers working on the same knowledge, but using different language?
- Some people reject the healing ministry as '*A merely emotional form of evangelical Christianity.*' Comment.

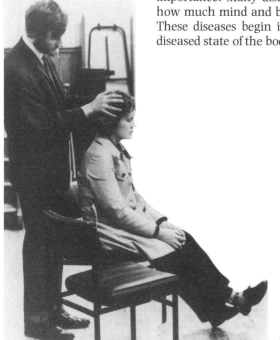

Faith healing

# 'We did not feel foreign'

ALTHOUGH we had been told much about Lourdes it was difficult to know what to expect, but we were in no way disappointed.

We came down with an English pilgrimage by train. The first sight of Lourdes that immediately strikes those arriving by train is the Grotto and Basilica.

It had been arranged before that we should go to work in one of the hospitals, and we immediately felt at home as all the English-speaking nuns and helpers offered to help us in any way they could.

Another extraordinary thing is that we did not feel like foreigners. Because there are so many nationalities in Lourdes all at the same time one would imagine that language would be a barrier, but this was not the case; everyone made a great effort and, even if it was just by sign language, we would be able to communicate. A smile to a sick person often means a lot, and they would smile back.

We worked in the hospital for a week and found that the atmosphere was an extremely happy one within the pilgrimages. Everyone was ready to help and no one felt as though they were a stranger. The sick pilgrims were often laughing and joking with us and would help each other.

As the pilgrimages left we did not find that the sick people were disappointed because they had not been physically cured; they were happy because they had found fellowship one with another and thus found the strength to live with their illnesses.

*(Catherine Lewis on a visit to Lourdes)*

Pilgrims at Lourdes

Find out about Lourdes, the French shrine where the sick go, seeking to be cured.

Father O'Mahony and a fellow worker in the Wayside team pack medical supplies for Poland

The **Pentecostal Movement** is growing in the churches. Sometimes called the 'charismatic renewal' it has revived an interest in the New Testament gifts of the Holy Spirit. These gifts include healing and speaking with tongues. Find out more about the Movement.

## Medical profession baffled by cures says obstetrician

# BMA consultant talks of 'miracle' cures

### by Terence Sheehy

"THERE ARE an increasing number of cases known to members of the British Medical profession whose cures cannot be explained other than by the word miraculous," says Mr Rex Gardner in the latest *British Medical Journal.* Mr Gardner, Chairman of the British Medical Association's Sunderland Branch, consultant obstetrician and gynaecologist, and a doctor for 32 years, has just published his views on prayer and healing in the doctors' "bible".

# C10 Prayer

### Some facts

Christians have always found it important to find time for prayer. How do people pray? And what happens when they pray? For most Christians personal prayer means stopping activity and finding time to be still enough to become aware of the invisible world. Metropolitan Anthony (Bloom) writes:

> *Prayer is born of the discovery that the world has depths; that we are...*
> *immersed in and penetrated by invisible things. And this invisible world*
> *is both the presence of God, the supreme reality, and our own deepest*
> *truth.*

In Luke's Gospel Jesus is seen to pray at important moments of his life.

> *At that time Jesus went up a hill to pray and spent the whole night*
> *there praying to God.*
>
> Luke 6:12

It is natural for Christians to do the same. Baptisms, marriages and funerals are obvious examples, but other events are remembered in prayer too. The Roman Catholic Church, for example, has *seven* sacraments of life. Find out what they are. Do all Christian denominations have sacraments?

Christians are encouraged to pray with the community. They meet most regularly to celebrate the Eucharist, in memory of the Last Supper of Jesus. In the Church of England this is the Communion Service; in the Roman Catholic Church it is the Mass; in the Orthodox Churches it is the Sacred Liturgy.

The four main types of prayer can be recalled by using the word **ACTS.** Adoration, Contribution, Thanksgiving, Supplication.

### Ask yourself

- Prayer of supplication (asking) presents a difficulty. What happens when God is asked to change a situation? Does he? Can he?
- If you think God *could* heal a sick child in answer to a prayer, how do you explain why many sick children die every day?
- If you think God can't alter how things are, why pray at all?

Many people use a Gospel text as a starting point for their prayer. They reflect on the scene and apply it to their own lives. We'll take the *transfiguration* of Jesus (Luke 9: 28 ff) as an example.

*Orthodox Christians* will reflect on the transfiguration by standing silently before its icon. An icon is a religious painting. Icon in Greek means an image. Eastern Christians believe that these paintings reveal the presence of God. They put the prayerful individual in contact with God in something of the way that Christ did. Paul called Christ the icon of God: *'In him we see the God who can't be seen.'* (Colossians 1:15)

In 1980, the Catholic bishops of *El Salvador* wrote a letter to all their people. They ended it with a reflection on the same Gospel scene. They described Moses, Elijah, Peter, James and John as men *'capable of fighting, but who preferred peace to war.'*

In a similar way Rowan Williams uses the transfiguration scene to reflect upon today's world. He notes that when the transfigured Jesus leaves the mountain he is confronted by a boy possessed by a demon. Williams comments that the 6th August, the churches' Feast of the Transfiguration, has become *Hiroshima Day.*

> *Suicidal, diabolic sickness still waits at the bottom of the mountain, though now there are more bodies to look at.*

> *Jesus channelled the aggression of those temperaments towards a rich work of construction, of building up justice and peace in the world. Let us ask the Divine Patron of El Salvador to transfigure in the same way the rich potential of this people.*

Icon of the transfiguration

**A Bible Prayer**

Father, I thank you for this gospel story
  which illustrates so well Christ's sovereignty.
I believe, Lord, that in everything he says and does
  he lights up and fulfils the law and the prophets;
  and it is enough to listen to him.
For Jesus is your Christ,
  even though death and dereliction
  are waiting for him in Jerusalem.
It will be dark there,
  and on another hill, shaped like a skull,
  two other men will be beside him.
From his unclothed body no light will radiate;
  and even you, Father, will be silent,
  except for the one Word you will be saying to us
  in the tremendous love of Jesus crucified.

                 Peter De Rosa

# C11  Crime and forgiveness

## Some facts

Why do people turn to crime? Statistics show that in the most developed countries (Europe, N. America) the crime rate goes up year after year. Why? The following are sometimes given as causes:

| | | | |
|---|---|---|---|
| Poverty | Revenge | Unemployment | Greed |
| Boredom | Overcrowding in cities | Social inadequacy | |

It has often been pointed out that an unusually high percentage of prisoners in Britain are Roman Catholics. Why should this be so? Could it be connected with the fact that the largest Catholic communities are situated in deprived inner-city areas.

*Forgive them, Father! They don't know what they are doing.*

Luke 23:34

*'Oh, come off it, Father. How can I believe that God forgives me when people don't? The magistrate didn't forgive me! And people will always remember that he sent me away. People* never *forgive you.'*

These are the words of a young offender to the prison chaplain. What could the chaplain reply to them?

Some sixth formers recently asked prison chaplains to question their congregation about their beliefs. It emerged that although prison life gave them the opportunity to think more deeply about their lives, and although many found their religion a source of comfort, most prisoners felt that their churches had written them off, and were totally unconcerned about them. Is this a fair criticism?

## Ask yourself

- If a member of your family went to prison would you welcome him/her back home?
- If you were an employer, would you employ someone with a prison record?
- Are there any types of criminal who should *never* be released? If you believe there are, does this mean that these people are never forgiven?
- What do you feel about the death penalty? Can a practising Christian support the return of the death penalty? (A Christian believes that all life is sacred.)

A prison cell

Ann is in prison for shoplifting. She had turned to this crime when her alcoholic husband began to take her housekeeping money and the children's allowance.

Desperate for help, she went into the Catholic church, lit a candle by a statue and begged God for help. She was determined not to steal again. She knew it was her last chance with the Law. But she had no food in the house. Her three children were hungry. She went by the supermarket. The temptation was too much.

'*How can I believe in your God of love?*' she asked the nun prison visitor. '*I asked for bread and he gave me prison. And my children are taken from me.*'

What would be your reply to Ann?

Discarded police helmets after the Libyan Embassy siege, April 1984

## Punishment

Why are people sent to prison?
(a) to punish them?
(b) to deter others from crime?
(c) to reform them?
(d) a bit of each?

Police dealing with trouble at Norwich City football club

## Overcrowding

Ex-prisoners say that very often the real punishment begins on the day they are released. They often leave prison with nowhere permanent to live, no job, no family (or a broken family), no change of clothes, very little money, no stamps on the insurance card, no reference from the last employer, and *no hope.*

# Vandalism and the inner city

# C12 World unity

### Some facts

Young people are usually the most idealistic about the world. A theologian, W. Salters Sterling, recognizing this, observed that ideals for a united world can be identified with the ideals of Christianity.

*I identify six points of similarity between the crisis among the young today and the crisis which is always present in Christianity. They are: (a) there is the same ecumenical vision—a blessing to all nations; (b) there is a prophetic concern for justice and righteousness; (c) there is a determination, as with Abraham, to make history, and not just to live under and through history; (d) there is a willingness to go out, like Abraham, 'not knowing whithersoever he went'; (e) there is a desire, like that of Christ, that living should be abundant living; (f) there is a consciousness of responsibility for the proper dominion of man over the natural world and its resources. It may be that I am too optimistic—I hope not, for I sense a great potential in the crisis among the young.*

*Concilium, 9, 5*

Is this what Isaiah and Luke mean?

*All mankind will see God's salvation.*

Luke 3:6

### Ask yourself

- People find it very difficult to live in isolation, but even more difficult to live in harmony with others. Take a look at the groups to which you belong: Family, School, Youth Club, Parish, etc. Make a list of all the tensions that can exist in these groups. Why do these tensions exist?
- Of course, the larger the community the more difficult it will be to create harmony. We speak today of living in a *global village*. This means that we all accept we are citizens of *one world*, knowing each other far better than we did, depending on each other for food and industrial goods, and appreciating each other's riches.

  Find out what you can about the following international bodies which try to promote harmony
  1. The United Nations
  2. The European Economic Community (Common Market)
  3. The British Commonwealth
  4. The International Committee for the Olympic Games.

Over the centuries, Christianity has divided into sects or denominations. At the beginning of this century many who were scandalized by these divisions began to seek ways of coming together. Their efforts became known as the *Ecumenical* (worldwide) *Movement*.

Does this 'ecumenism' mean that Christian denominations should abandon their individuality and accept a *common* faith and practice? That seems unlikely. Some say it is quite unnecessary.

If Jesus, according to Luke, welcomed outsiders and outcasts, presumably his followers will recognize the loving creativity of God at work in ALL PEOPLE, whether they are Protestant or Catholic, indeed whether they are Christian or not.

These children in Peru are seeing books for the first time in their lives. They were sent to them by the children of St John's First School, Norwich, who have adopted them.

Bob Geldof's **Live Aid** is a striking example of worldwide co-operation.

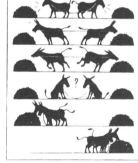

CO-OPERATION

IS BETTER THAN CONFLICT

*Taizé is an extraordinary community in France, devoted to Christian unity. It attracts thousands of young people every year. Find out about it.*

What is the World Council of Churches? What has it achieved since its beginning?

ONE WORLD

A BULLETIN ON WORLD DEVELOPMENT AND JUSTICE

Published by Trócaire, the Catholic Agency for World Development

*All Adam's sons
Are limbs of one another
each of the self same
Substance as his brother.*

Sa'adi, a Persian Poet

# WORLD COUNCIL OF CHURCHES

# A last word

### Friday Morning

1　*It was on a Friday morning*
　*That they took me from the cell,*
　*And I saw they had a carpenter*
　*To crucify as well.*
　*You can blame it on to Pilate,*
　*You can blame it on the Jews,*
　*You can blame it on the Devil,*
　*It's God I accuse.*
　*It's God they ought to crucify*
　*Instead of you and me,*
　*I said to the carpenter*
　*A-hanging on the tree.*

2　*You can blame it on to Adam,*
　*You can blame it on to Eve,*
　*You can blame it on the Apple,*
　*But that I can't believe.*
　*It was God that made the Devil*
　*And the Woman and the Man,*
　*And there wouldn't be an Apple*
　*If it wasn't in the plan.*
　*It's God they ought to crucify*
　*Instead of you and me,*
　*I said to the carpenter*
　*A-hanging on the tree.*

3　*Now Barabbas was a killer*
　*And they let Barabbas go.*
　*But you are being crucified*
　*For nothing, here below.*
　*But God is up in heaven*
　*And he doesn't do a thing:*
　*With a million angels watching,*
　*And they never move a wing.*
　*It's God they ought to crucify*
　*Instead of you and me,*
　*I said to the carpenter*
　*A-hanging on the tree.*

4　*To hell with Jehovah,*
　*To the carpenter I said,*
　*I wish that a carpenter*
　*Had made the world instead.*
　*Goodbye and good luck to you,*
　*Our ways will soon divide.*
　*Remember me in heaven,*
　*The man you hung beside.*
　*It's God they ought to crucify*
　*Instead of you and me,*
　*I said to the carpenter*
　*A-hanging on the tree.*

Sydney Carter's version of Luke 23:42
(pub. Stainer & Bell Ltd)